The Traveling Minister's Handbook

The Traveling Minister's Handbook

Marvin Yoder

FAITH LIBRARY PUBLICATIONS

Second Edition
First Printing 2000

ISBN # 0-89276-963-7

In the U.S. write:
Kenneth Hagin Ministries
P.O. Box 50126
Tulsa, OK 74150-0126
1-888-28-FAITH
www.rhema.org

In Canada write:
Kenneth Hagin Ministries
P.O. Box 335, Station D
Etobicoke (Toronto), Ontario
Canada, M9A 4X3

C ONTENTS

SECTION VI: PROPER ETHICS IN THE TRAVELING MINISTRY

SECTION VII: DEVELOPING YOUR TRAVELING MINISTRY

SECTION VIII: PREACHING EFFECTIVELY

SECTION IX: SPECIAL KINDS OF TRAVELING MINISTRIES

A FINAL WORD

A B O U T   T H E
A U T H O R

Marvin Yoder grew up in the Old Order Amish Church, driving a horse and buggy and having no car, radio, or television in his home. Marvin was born again as a ten-year-old boy, and years later, God called him into the ministry.

After graduating from Rhema Bible Training Center in 1984, Marvin pastored several denominational and nondenominational churches in Kansas and Illinois. He also served as Dean of Academics at a Bible school in the Midwest for five years.

Marvin has traveled extensively throughout the United States, teaching in churches, conducting seminars, and holding Holy Ghost meetings. He has also taken missions trips to Canada and the Czech Republic. Marvin has served as the Assistant Dean of Rhema and as a Rhema instructor since 1998.

Marvin has authored several books and study guides, and he and his wife, Leah, have been married since 1979 and have three daughters.

Marvin Yoder has produced a "here's how" for the traveling minister. Here are the "nuts and bolts" of the traveling ministry coupled with a solid foundation of character and integrity. It would take considerable time to collect and reproduce the cutting-edge information provided in Yoder's best-selling handbook...an indispensable guide.

William V. Crouch
President, Van Crouch Communications
Minister, Conference Speaker, Trainer

I wish The Traveling Minister's Handbook had been available to me thirty years ago. Wise is the person who learns from others' counsel and builds upon the wisdom and experience of those who have traveled the road ahead of him. Save yourself a lot of time, money, and frustration by using this amazing resource. You will thank God you did!

Len Mink
President, Len Mink Ministries
Worship Leader and Psalmist, Evangelist, Creator of "Gospel Duck"

The Traveling Minister's Handbook is a must for anyone contemplating any type of itinerant ministry. Rev. Marvin Yoder provides excellent examples of forms and letters that an evangelist or any type of traveling minister could use in doing the work of the ministry. This volume alone could help a fledgling ministry become a successful ministry if the reader would apply the information found within. I heartily recommend this volume to anyone who feels called to a traveling ministry.

Dr. James Tollett
Associate Professor of Practical Theology,
Director of Field and Assessment, Oral Roberts University

F O R E W O R D

The Traveling Minister's Handbook is the most comprehensive resource for the traveling minister that I have ever seen. It is well-organized and covers every aspect of the traveling ministry. In addition, its message of excellence, ethics, and integrity is very important to the Body of Christ.

When I was in Bible school, nothing like this handbook was available. As a result, when I began my traveling ministry, I had to learn everything in this book through my own trial and error!

This book is a "must-read" for all traveling ministers.

Kenneth Hagin Jr.

Rev. Kenneth Hagin Jr.

EDITOR'S PREFACE

Numerous companies and organizations are mentioned in this book, and every effort was made to prove each one reputable at the time of this writing. However, the author, all contributing individuals, and Faith Library Publications cannot be held liable for the future performance and actions of any of the individuals, companies, or organizations mentioned in this book.

Every effort has been made to verify that all the addresses and telephone numbers mentioned in this book are correct. However, addresses and telephone numbers do change from time to time. If necessary, please call information services to obtain the current information.

PREFACE

I am excited to be able to present this book to the Body of Christ. Having had the opportunity to both pastor and travel in the Body of Christ, I have seen a tremendous need for resource material to help those who are in the traveling ministry. Because of the diversity in traveling ministries, one minister may choose to do something in a different way than another traveling minister would do it. However, there are many principles and goals that can be shared by all traveling ministers.

All traveling ministers must be accountable and conduct themselves according to the godly principles contained in the Scriptures. These principles will help traveling ministers to maintain correct motives, conduct themselves ethically, and know how to minister effectively as they travel in the Body of Christ.

Traveling ministers must know their place and function in the Body of Christ. They are to support pastors and help them build the local church. They must be promoters of the vision the pastor has received from God. A vital and valuable part of the Body of Christ, traveling ministers are not inferior to pastors, nor are they superior to pastors. Traveling ministers and pastors should labor side by side, working for a common goal — to help lead the Body of Christ into growth, strength, stability, wholeness, and maturity.

This book has been a joint effort on the part of a number of individuals who were willing to share from their areas of expertise. In writing this book, I have had the privilege of working with traveling ministers, pastors, attorneys, various individuals in supportive roles, and various professional people. Many people have contributed to this book, and I am grateful to each of them.

I could not have put this book together without the invaluable information I received while attending Rhema Bible Training Center in Broken Arrow, Oklahoma. Rhema provided me with the finest education and ministerial training available.

I also want to express my thanks to all the people at Faith Library Publications; they were wonderful to work with. They supplied what was necessary to transform this information from original manuscript to the book you now have in your hands.

My prayer is that this book will be a blessing and an encouragement to you as you pursue the call of God upon your life. God bless you as you endeavor to fulfill your God-given ministry.

— Marvin Yoder

Taking a Look at the Traveling Ministry

1

So You Think You Want To Travel?

Today there are many people involved in some type of traveling ministry. They are functioning in various capacities — as evangelists, teachers, musicians, missionaries, exhorters, or prophets, to name a few. Even some pastors travel at times to other churches, various conferences, and to foreign countries on short-term missions trips.

The traveling ministry is a mystery to most people. Most lay people, Bible school students, and ministers do not understand it. The call, the role, and the function of the traveling minister is very important, yet it is often

1. Write down the scripture upon which your call into the ministry is based.

_____

_____

_____

_____

_____

_____

_____

_____

_____

_____

_____

_____

_____

_____

_____

ACTS 26:19
Whereupon, O king Agrippa, I was not disobedient unto the heavenly vision.

misunderstood. Some of the most often asked questions include:

- How do I know I am supposed to be a traveling minister?
- How do I get started in the traveling ministry?
- How do I schedule meetings?
- What do I need to get started?
- Where do I get started with my traveling ministry?

There are many people who would like to be in the traveling ministry. Some people even feel called of God to start a traveling ministry, but they have no idea how to do it.

ESTABLISH WHETHER OR NOT YOU ARE CALLED

One of the first things a person must do in starting a traveling ministry is determine if they are really called to be a traveling minister. Having a desire is necessary; however, that alone is not enough. A person must hear from God as to what his or her function is in the Body of Christ, no matter what ministry he or she wants to be involved in.

Here is an acronym that will help you to see what it means to be called by God into a certain ministry.

C - Chosen by God

A - Available to minister

L - Loyal to the will of God

L - Loving toward all people

The Apostle Paul received the call of God on the road to Damascus. He then established himself in that call and never forgot it. When Paul had to stand before King Agrippa, he declared his faithfulness to the call of God by saying, "Whereupon, O king Agrippa, I was not disobedient unto the heavenly vision"(Acts 26:19).

The call of God is the beginning. You cannot enter into the traveling ministry just because you want to do it. Desire alone is not enough reason to have a traveling ministry.

To be successful in the traveling ministry, it is necessary to know beyond a shadow of doubt that this is what God wants you to do. Knowing that God Himself has directed you to be in the traveling ministry will enable you to stay faithful to that call. When you are living and functioning in the call of God you will find:

- Peace
- Creativity
- Initiative
- Strength
- Fortitude
- Anointing
- Eternal fruit

Without the call of God to be in the traveling ministry, you may encounter unnecessary hardships and difficulties. It is important that a person establishes the will

2. Write down your past experience in the traveling ministry.

_____

_____

_____

_____

_____

_____

_____

_____

_____

_____

_____

_____

_____

_____

_____

_____

_____

_____

_____

_____

_____

_____

3. Evaluate your traveling ministry in the following areas:

Have you sowed much and reaped little?

Yes No

☐ ☐

Do you experience continual hard times with no fruit to show for it?

Yes No

☐ ☐

Are you having a lot of frustration?

Yes No

☐ ☐

Are you worn out physically, mentally, or emotionally?

Yes No

☐ ☐

of God for his life and then operates faithfully in it. People who step into a ministry they are not called to be in may experience:

- Sowing or giving much and reaping very little for it.
- Continual hard times with no fruit to show for it.
- Much frustration, despair, anger, or hopelessness.
- Being worn out physically, mentally, and emotionally.

THE TRAVELING MINISTRY IS SCRIPTURAL

Looking at what Jesus said and did during His earthly ministry reveals that the traveling ministry helps to fulfill the Great Commission.

MATTHEW 28:18-20
And Jesus came and spake unto them, saying, All power is given unto me in heaven and in earth.
Go ye therefore, and teach all nations, baptizing them in the name of the Father, and of the Son, and of the Holy Ghost.
Teaching them to observe all things whatsoever I have commanded you: and, lo, I am with you alway, even unto the end of the world. Amen.

Jesus Himself traveled from place to place during His ministry.

MATTHEW 4:23

And Jesus went about all Galilee, teaching in their synagogues, and preaching the gospel of the kingdom, and healing all manner of sickness and all manner of disease among the people.

MATTHEW 9:35

And Jesus went about all the cities and villages, teaching in their synagogues, and preaching the gospel of the kingdom, and healing every sickness and every disease among the people.

MATTHEW 11:1

And it came to pass, when Jesus had made an end of commanding his twelve disciples, he departed thence to teach and to preach in their cities.

MATTHEW 19:1

And it came to pass, that when Jesus had finished these sayings, he departed from Galilee, and came into the coasts of Judaea beyond Jordan.

Jesus sent His disciples to travel to various places.

LUKE 9:1,2

Then he called his twelve disciples together, and gave them power and authority over all devils, and to cure diseases.
And he sent them to preach the kingdom of God, and to heal the sick.

4. In the traveling ministry have you experienced:

Yes No

☐ ☐ Creativity

☐ ☐ Strength

☐ ☐ Initiative

☐ ☐ Fortitude

☐ ☐ Anointing

☐ ☐ Eternal fruit

Personal Notes

_____

_____

_____

_____

_____

_____

_____

_____

_____

_____

_____

_____

_____

Personal Notes

LUKE 10:1
After these things the Lord appointed other seventy also, and sent them two and two before his face into every city and place, whither he himself would come.

Several of the apostles mentioned in the Book of Acts traveled in order to fulfill their ministry.

- Peter traveled in various parts of the Middle East.
- Philip traveled to Samaria.
- Paul traveled the known world.
- Barnabas traveled with Paul.
- Luke traveled with Paul.
- Timothy traveled with Paul.

CONCLUSION

The traveling ministry is certainly very scriptural, but you must have the call of God in order to be successful in it. Otherwise it may just be "good works" and not part of God's specific will for your life.

2

Personal Glamour Or God's Glory?

The visible part of the traveling ministry is a very small part compared to all that has to be done behind the scenes in order to have a successful traveling ministry. What most people see in the traveling ministry is very appealing and desirable.

If a person goes into the traveling ministry based only upon what he sees, he won't have the stamina to remain in the traveling ministry. It takes the invisible resources and abilities of God to stay strong emotionally, mentally, and spiritually.

Write down what you thought the traveling ministry was like prior to reading this lesson.

_____

_____

_____

_____

_____

_____

_____

_____

_____

_____

_____

_____

_____

_____

_____

_____

_____

_____

People watch the traveling minister receive the attention and honor of being a special guest and the special privileges that are extended to him. Therefore numerous people want to get into the traveling ministry based upon what they see rather than realizing what actually is involved in conducting a traveling ministry.

All that most people see in the traveling ministry is:

- The glamour of being treated as a guest.
- The honor and respect given to the traveling minister.
- The anointing of God that traveling ministers use to effectively minister to people.
- The privileges that are given to traveling ministers.
- The offerings that traveling ministers receive.

A REAL VISION FROM GOD FOR THE TRAVELING MINISTRY

A person called into the traveling ministry must have a real spiritual call or vision of God in order to minister effectively. The vision of God will produce:

- **A mandate to go.** Some traveling ministers I know did not have a desire to travel, but God said, "Go ye..." This enabled them to continue ministering even when they did not feel like it.
- **A desire to serve the churches and the people.** The heart of God is to give. As you follow God's

will, your priority will be to see how much you can give instead of how much you can receive.

- **An anointing to confirm the call, preach the Word, produce effective ministry, and get the work done.** When a person has the anointing of God, the power of God is available to minister the Word effectively, and people's lives will experience freedom and change.

- **A grace to travel and be gone from home.** It takes God's grace to leave home time after time, stay in strange places, and minister to people you do not even know. You must remember that God knows them and loves them so much that He will send someone like yourself to share the Good News of Jesus Christ with them.

- **A guiding path on which to continue.** Often when I wanted to quit, I remembered the words Jesus spoke in my call, "Go into all the world, and preach the Gospel…" Those words convinced me that I was in the perfect will of God and enabled me to keep going.

- **An endurance and strength to "fight the good fight of faith" and to finish the work.** Philippians 4:13 says, "I can do all things through Christ which strengtheneth me."

- **A love for the people to whom you are sent.** Jesus was moved with compassion and this motivated

ACTS 9:15,16

But the Lord said unto him, Go thy way: for he is a chosen vessel unto me, to bear my name before the Gentiles, and kings, and the children of Israel:

For I will shew him how great things he must suffer for my name's sake.

Personal Notes

_____

_____

_____

_____

_____

_____

_____

_____

_____

_____

_____

_____

_____

_____

EVALUATION AND REVIEW

Did you have visions of glamour and fame about the traveling ministry?

Yes No

☐ ☐

Did you base your decision on the visible part of the traveling ministry?

Yes No

☐ ☐

Were you focused on obeying God's will and experiencing the glory of God?

Yes No

☐ ☐

Did you have a correct picture of what the traveling ministry actually entails?

Yes No

☐ ☐

Him to minister to people. As you allow the compassion of God to move you to travel from place to place, you will become a vessel that God's love can flow through. If you will learn to be a vessel or channel of God's love, you will become an indispensable part of the Kingdom of God.

THE TRUTH ABOUT THE TRAVELING MINISTRY

HABAKKUK 2:2,3

And the Lord answered me, and said, Write the vision, and make it plain upon tables, that he may run that readeth it.

For the vision is yet for an appointed time, but at the end it shall speak, and not lie: though it tarry, wait for it; because it will surely come, it will not tarry.

- It usually takes 2-5 years to be full-time in the traveling ministry.
- If you cannot handle rejection, abuse, or misuse, you won't make it in the traveling ministry.
- If you don't like sales, you may not be successful in the traveling ministry.
- Marketing is necessary in the traveling ministry. Jesus used the advertising methods of the times He lived in to market His ministry (Luke 10:1 NIV).

- Contacting and developing relationships with other ministers is a constant necessity. Remember that relationships are very important in the ministry.
- Sometimes you may need to travel long hours to get where you're scheduled to preach. In times like that, you may wonder why in the world you are in the traveling ministry.
- As a traveling minister, you will find yourself repeatedly packing and unpacking clothes, books, tapes, equipment, etc.
- Meeting schedules and deadlines promptly is an absolute must in the traveling ministry.
- Scheduling meetings with churches will seem like a never-ending task.
- You may spend many lonely hours in a motel room.
- Working more than forty hours a week is necessary in order to be successful in the traveling ministry. If you are a "nine-to-five" person, the traveling ministry may not be for you.
- On top of all the things you have to do while you are traveling, you also come home to office work that has been waiting for you. Some things can be done by others who are helping you, but there are some things that only you can do.
- Trying to meet unrealistic expectations of people is a pressure that probably every traveling minister deals with. A traveling minister must learn to

Personal Notes

Personal Notes

_____

_____

_____

_____

_____

_____

_____

_____

_____

_____

_____

_____

_____

_____

_____

_____

_____

_____

_____

_____

spend sufficient time with God and His Word to overcome the temptation of trying to do something that just pleases people.

- As a traveling minister, you will experience times when you are trying to obey both God and the pastor of the church where you are ministering.
- At times you may not be able to see any visible evidence to confirm that you are in the will of God. During those times, you must remember that God has sent you forth.
- You must be willing to forfeit the glitter of recognition in exchange for the glory of God, which is found only at the place of obedience. Philip was someone who experienced God's miraculous power because he obeyed God's direction. By the direction of the Holy Spirit, Philip went to Samaria and experienced great revival. People were born again, healed, and received the baptism with the Holy Spirit. Then the Spirit of God told Philip to leave the revival in Samaria and go to the desert. Because Philip was obedient to go, he again experienced God's miraculous power in manifestation (Acts 8:26).

For This Purpose...

Taking time to determine the purpose of your ministry is necessary in order to know if you are to be in some type of traveling ministry.

WHY ARE YOU IN THE TRAVELING MINISTRY?

Some people are in the traveling ministry because of desire. Others are in a traveling ministry for the money. Still others are in a traveling ministry to build a name for themselves and are pursuing fame and recognition.

Write down the original word you received from God regarding ministry.

_____

_____

_____

_____

_____

_____

_____

_____

_____

_____

_____

_____

_____

_____

_____

_____

_____

Finally, some people try the traveling ministry because they don't know what else to do.

Your motives are more important than your actions. Why you do something is more important than what you do. The value of what you do is determined by why you're doing it. So you must know your purpose in ministry because this will help you have the right motives.

The Apostle Paul said that Christ is preached for many reasons.

> **PHILIPPIANS 1:15-17**
> **Some indeed preach Christ even of envy and strife; and some also of good will:**
> **The one preach Christ of contention, not sincerely, supposing to add affliction to my bonds:**
> **But the other of love, knowing that I am set for the defense of the gospel.**

THE ORIGINAL WORD FROM GOD OFTEN REVEALS OUR PURPOSE

Seasons in our lives and ministries may change, and the emphasis of your message may shift, but certain aspects of your original call will never be outgrown.

In Paul's life we can see that he went through various seasons, the emphasis of his ministry changed, and even the ministry offices that he functioned in changed. But all of the changes were necessary so that Paul could fulfill his purpose which was revealed in the original word God spoke to him.

Often there is a natural assignment or method God wants us to use in fulfilling a spiritual purpose. For example, God may tell you to start singing Gospel music. But, what He really wants is the fruit that will come when people are exposed to the words and the anointing by which you sing.

Your calling and purpose will determine the methods you are to use and what kind of anointing God will give you.

GOD HAS VARIOUS PURPOSES FOR DIFFERENT INDIVIDUALS

Jesus had a purpose for manifesting in the flesh and in going to Calvary. He corrected His disciples by reminding them of His purpose for coming into the earth.

LUKE 9:56
For the Son of man is not come to destroy men's lives, but to save them....

Later the Apostle John wrote a similar statement in one of his epistles concerning Jesus' purpose for manifesting in the flesh on earth.

ACTS 9:15
But the Lord said unto him, Go thy way: for he is a chosen vessel unto me, to bear my name before the Gentiles, and kings, and the children of Israel.

Personal Notes

_____

_____

_____

_____

_____

_____

_____

_____

_____

_____

_____

_____

_____

_____

What purposes are revealed in that original word from God that you are to accomplish?

_____

_____

_____

_____

_____

_____

_____

_____

_____

_____

_____

_____

_____

_____

_____

_____

_____

1 JOHN 3:8
...For this purpose the Son of God was manifested, that he might destroy the works of the devil.

Paul knew the purpose to which he was called. He received his original word on the Damascus Road, and his whole ministry after that reflected that word. Years later when he told his Damascus Road experience with God to King Agrippa, he again stated his purpose in ministry by stating what God had told him that day.

ACTS 26:16-18
But rise, and stand upon thy feet: for I have appeared unto thee for this purpose, to make thee a minister and a witness both of these things which thou hast seen, and of those things in the which I will appear unto thee;
Delivering thee from the people, and from the Gentiles, unto whom now I send thee,
To open their eyes, and to turn them from darkness to light, and from the power of Satan unto God, that they may receive forgiveness of sins, and inheritance among them which are sanctified by faith that is in me.

Paul said he had fulfilled the purpose God had called him to. Notice that Paul did not attempt to complete someone else's purpose in life — he concentrated on God's purpose for his own life.

2 TIMOTHY 4:7

I have fought a good fight, I have finished MY COURSE, I have kept the faith.

DO NOT COMPARE YOURSELF WITH ANOTHER PERSON

Whatever your purpose, realize that God has appointed *you* to do it. Do not compare yourself with others who may not have a traveling ministry for the same purpose. Do what God tells you to do and you will fulfill your purpose in ministry.

You do not have to answer to God for another person's calling and purpose. But you do have to give an account concerning what you did with God's call and purpose for your life and ministry. God has given you a certain race to run, and no one else can run it for you, nor can you run someone else's course.

As George Barna said, "God's vision for your ministry is like a fingerprint: there is no other one exactly like it."

Because people have different callings and purposes that God has given to them, it is not wise to compare yourself with anyone else. If you are going to compare yourself with something, evaluate yourself in the light of God's call and purpose on your life.

Have you been comparing yourself with other traveling ministers and their purpose?

Yes No

☐ ☐

Are you concentrating on fulfilling God's purpose for your life?

Yes No

☐ ☐

Personal Notes

_____

_____

_____

_____

_____

_____

_____

_____

_____

_____

_____

Personal Notes

_____

_____

_____

_____

_____

_____

_____

_____

_____

_____

_____

_____

_____

_____

_____

_____

_____

_____

_____

2 CORINTHIANS 10:12

For we dare not make ourselves of the number, or compare ourselves with some that commend themselves: but they measuring themselves by themselves, and comparing themselves among themselves, are not wise.

The traveling ministry is usually a "niche ministry" in that it specializes in a certain area of ministry. As you travel from church to church, you will probably notice that God seems to use you in certain areas more than in other areas. That is another reason why you should avoid comparing yourself with other traveling ministers. Stay with the area that God uses you in the best — that is an indicator of the purpose God has for your ministry.

4

Identifying Your Anointing

The word "anointing" comes from the Greek word "chrisma," which means an unguent, a smearing, or a special endowment or unction of the Holy Spirit.

At the beginning of His ministry, Jesus made the announcement that the Spirit of God was upon Him and had anointed Him to carry out His earthly ministry (Luke 4:18). Jesus had the Greater One, the Holy Spirit, with Him so that He could minister effectively to the people. This is one of the reasons for the success of His earthly ministry.

LUKE 4:18

The Spirit of the Lord is upon me, because he hath anointed me to preach the gospel to the poor; he hath sent me to heal the brokenhearted, to preach deliverance to the captives, and re-covering of sight to the blind, to set at liberty them that are bruised.

Personal Notes

_____

_____

_____

_____

_____

_____

_____

_____

_____

_____

_____

_____

_____

ACTS 10:38

How God anointed Jesus of Nazareth with the Holy Ghost and with power: who went about doing good, and healing all that were oppressed of the devil; for God was with him.

Jesus was sent by God the Father to the earth in the form of a man to provide redemption for all mankind. In order to successfully carry out the will of the Father, Jesus was anointed by the Holy Spirit.

THE CALL DETERMINES THE ANOINTING

Everyone who is called into the ministry is sent out in the same way that Jesus was sent by the Father. An individual receives the call of God according to the will of the Father. However, every minister of God also needs to be anointed by the Holy Spirit so that he or she can successfully obey the Father and minister effectively to people.

As you go where God sends you and do what God has told you to do, the anointing will be present and functioning. The anointing accompanies the call of God upon an individual's life. And the call of God on your life will determine the kind of anointing you will have.

EXAMPLE:

• Peter was anointed to go to the Jews.

• Paul was anointed to go to the Gentiles.

GALATIANS 2:7,8
But contrariwise, when they saw that the gospel of the uncircumcision was committed unto me, as the gospel of the circumcision was unto Peter;
(For he that wrought effectually in Peter to the apostleship of the circumcision, the same was mighty in me toward the Gentiles.)

Every person that is sent by God to do the work of the ministry will have a specific anointing to fulfill that call. Certain anointings do not come just because you want it or because you have someone lay hands upon you. The anointing comes with the call, and it is manifested as a person endeavors to accomplish God's purposes. That anointing will then increase as a person labors in the call that God has given to him or her.

LEARN TO 'FINE-TUNE' YOUR ANOINTING

EPHESIANS 4:11
And he gave some, apostles; and some, prophets; and some, evangelists; and some, pastors and teachers.

Into which office of the five-fold ministry are you called? Are you called to be in the pastoral ministry? Or are you called to be a teacher or evangelist? These are

1. List the ministry offices, if any, to which God has called you, using the list in Ephesians 4:11.

2. If you know, list the type of ministry to which God has called you. For example, if God called you to be a teacher, what type of teacher are you?

_____

_____

_____

_____

_____

_____

_____

_____

_____

_____

_____

_____

_____

_____

_____

questions that should be answered according to what God has spoken to your heart.

Usually a minister who is just beginning in the ministry is not called to function in the apostolic or prophetic ministry. These two ministry offices require a greater degree of maturity and responsibility than the other three ministry offices do. Even though a person may eventually function in the apostolic or prophetic office, God will usually start a person in an office that does not require as much maturity or responsibility.

For example, Paul was called of God to be an apostle to the Gentiles (Acts 9). However, he functioned in the ministry for a number of years before he was separated by the Holy Spirit to be an apostle (Acts 13).

Often people feel called of God into the ministry; however, they do not know what area of ministry or ministry office they have been called to be in. In order to be effective in ministry, a person must establish what office of the five-fold ministry he is called to. Again, God has to put a person there — a person cannot decide on his own what he wants to do.

Once you have established what ministry office you are called to, determine the type of ministry you have. In other words, how does God want you to carry out His call upon your life? People with the call of God into the same ministry office may function differently as they fulfill the call.

For example, if God called you into the office of a teacher, what type of teacher are you? How and where are you to function? Just because two people are both called into the office of a teacher does not mean that they will function or operate their ministry the same way. Here are some examples of how a person could function in the call of God as a teacher:

- A staff teacher in a local church
- A Bible school teacher
- An itinerant teacher
- A pastoral teacher
- A prophetic teacher
- A Sunday School teacher
- A children's ministry teacher

Another question that should be settled in the heart of a minister is what particular subjects has God anointed him to speak on? As you operate in your ministry, begin to notice what subjects God seems to anoint more than others. What topic of ministry can you minister more effectively to people? Here are some examples of some well-known ministers and the subjects or topics that they were anointed by God to function in.

1. Kenneth Hagin is anointed to minister on faith and healing.
2. Oral Roberts is anointed to minister on healing.
3. Lester Sumrall was anointed to minister on deliverance.

3. List the specific subjects God has especially anointed you to teach or preach in the Body of Christ.

_____

_____

_____

_____

_____

_____

_____

_____

_____

_____

_____

_____

_____

_____

_____

_____

_____

_____

4. What predominant methods did Jesus and the apostles consistently use when operating in a ministry similar to what you are called to do?

_____

_____

_____

_____

_____

_____

_____

_____

_____

_____

_____

_____

_____

_____

_____

4. Howard Carter was anointed to minister on the baptism with the Holy Spirit and the gifts of the Spirit.

Sometimes certain people will have a peculiar anointing to minister the Gospel. For example, I know of one individual who at times is anointed of God to blow on people and use a chopping motion with his hand behind the people, a symbol of cutting off things that hinder their walk with God. Sometimes a minister will put his coat on someone and the person is healed.

Jesus had some peculiar anointings at various times. He spit on an individual's eyes. His shadow healed people. People touched His garment and were healed. He put mud on another individual's eyes and the man could see.

However, a word of caution is in order here. Notice that while Jesus had these times when a peculiar anointing would come on Him, He did not make that His predominant pattern or method of ministry. These incidents were exceptions and not the usual methods that Jesus normally used. Most of the time when Jesus ministered, He spoke the Word of God and laid His hands upon the sick.

If God causes a peculiar anointing to come on you, minister in it when that anointing is there. However, that should not be the normal method or pattern of ministry for you, nor should you try to make that peculiar anointing manifest at another time. Let God determine the anointing that is upon your ministry. Learn to major on the predominant principles of ministry that Jesus and the apostles in the Book of Acts used consistently in their ministries.

Some pastors' anointings are not necessarily limited to their local flock. Some pastors have a message and anointing for the Body of Christ at large, therefore they may also travel some. So do not judge a pastor too harshly when you see him traveling.

However, some pastors travel so much that they are only in their local church on Sundays. How can a pastor take care of the people in his local church if he is not there?

A wise word to people functioning in the office of a pastor would be to not travel all the time. Even if God called a pastor to share his message with the Body of Christ at large, his predominant place of ministry should still be his local church. A balance to this issue is that a pastor probably needs to be in his local church more than he is traveling to other churches.

CONCLUSION

"Fine-tuning" the anointing God has given to you will cause you to:

- be more effective in the ministry.
- be less frustrated.
- see greater fruit from your labors.

Personal Notes

5

Supernatural Beginnings

How do you get started in the traveling ministry? If you take a look at the people that God used in the Bible, you see that each one was busy doing what he knew to do right up until the moment when God gave specific direction.

- Moses was tending sheep, and suddenly, a burning bush appeared. That incident propelled him into becoming the leader that God chose to lead the Israelites out of Egypt.

- Gideon was threshing wheat in a vat when an angel suddenly appeared to him. He received

PROVERBS 18:16

A man's gift maketh room for him, and bringeth him before great men.

Personal Notes

_____

_____

_____

_____

_____

_____

_____

_____

_____

_____

_____

_____

_____

_____

direction from God that caused him to be used of God and become one of the judges of Israel.

- Nehemiah was serving in the king's palace when God put a burden on his heart for the restoration of Jerusalem.

- Peter was a fisherman busy at his trade when Jesus came by and called him to become a fisher of men.

- Saul was involved in serving God according to Jewish religion, and suddenly, a bright light from Heaven appeared. From that moment, Saul's life was dramatically changed, and he was mightily used by God to reach the Gentiles for Christ.

- Zachariah was in the temple, fulfilling his duties according to the Law, when an angel suddenly appeared, telling him that he would have a son. Zachariah was to name him John the Baptist — the one who would foretell coming of Christ the Messiah.

God may not give you a vision, send an angel to appear to you, or cause a bush to catch on fire. But God will move in your life to enable you to do what He has called you to do. If God has called you into the traveling ministry, be faithful where you are. As you continue to trust in Him, God will provide the opportunity for you to be in the traveling ministry.

THE CALL OF GOD WILL PRODUCE THE OPPORTUNITY

Trust in the Lord to bring about your ministry. You may not know how to do what God has told you to do, but God can create the opportunity for you to operate in His calling. As a traveling minister, you have to stay faithful with what you are doing and allow God to open up more doors for you to minister.

PROVERBS 18:16
A man's gift maketh room for him, and bringeth him before great men.

Many people strain and strive too much to make the calling of God come to pass. It is true that you as the individual called by God have to get up and start doing something. At the same time, it is so important that you realize that your gift and call will make a place for you. Be confident about the gift God has placed inside of you. What God has placed inside you will come forth at the right time just as a plant bears fruit in season. You do not have to push yourself on others or step on others to get started in ministry.

ECCLESIASTES 3:1,11
To every thing there is a season, and a time to every purpose under the heaven....
He [God] **hath made every thing beautiful in his time....**

PROVERBS 3:5,6
Trust in the Lord with all thine heart; and lean not unto thine own understanding.
In all thy ways acknowledge him, and he shall direct thy paths.

Personal Notes

Personal Notes

Remember, there is a season for everything. Timing is very important in following God's instructions. When you move with God, you can experience His supernatural power in fulfilling His call upon your life. When you follow God's timing and direction, you will burst forth to do what God has called you to do as a flower bursts into full bloom.

JOHN 15:5
I am the vine, ye are the branches: He that abideth in me, and I in him, the same bringeth forth much fruit: for without me ye can do nothing.

Determine that you won't do anything unless God is in it. Doing what God has instructed you to do and refusing to be sidetracked is a secret to being successful. Let God put you over. As He directs you, be obedient, knowing that He will confirm your labors.

BE READY FOR 'SUDDENLY'

You can believe God for a supernatural breakthrough to start your ministry, but be ready to take advantage of the opportunity when it comes. Many times we wait and believe God for something, and suddenly, God moves on our behalf. For example, the disciples were in the Upper Room praying, knowing that God had called them into the ministry, when suddenly, on the Day of Pentecost, the Holy Spirit moved!

ACTS 2:1,2
And when the day of Pentecost was fully come, they were all with one accord in one place. And SUD-DENLY there came a sound from heaven as of a rushing mighty wind, and it filled all the house where they were sitting.

As you provide the willingness and obedience to the call, God will provide the breakthrough you need. Both your attitude and your actions are important in following God. I have met some people who were obedient to God's direction but were not very willing. They did not receive the blessings of God like they could have.

ISAIAH 1:19
If ye be WILLING AND OBEDIENT, ye shall eat the good of the land.

Everyone who is in the traveling ministry has a different story. In my case, I had resigned from pastoring a church, knowing that I was to start traveling in the Body of Christ. I waited for approximately six months, knowing what I was supposed to do but not knowing how to get started.

Personal Notes

Personal Notes

_____

_____

_____

_____

_____

_____

_____

_____

_____

_____

_____

_____

_____

_____

_____

_____

PSALM 75:6,7
For promotion cometh nei-
ther from the east, nor from
the west, nor from the south.
But God is the judge: he put-
teth down one, and setteth
up another.

God gave me the opportunity to be head usher in a crusade that a well-known minister was conducting in my city. During the course of the crusade, I seated a number of ministers in a special section which had been provided for them. One of those ministers asked me to speak in his church. That started the traveling ministry for me. And I have built upon the opportunity that God provided.

Billy Graham's big opportunity came when a newspaper editor instructed his staff to "push Graham." This gave Rev. Graham exposure throughout America.

Some supernatural breakthroughs only seem supernatural in retrospect. At the time it may have seemed that a very ordinary course of events took place, but those events created supernatural breakthroughs and opportunities for ministry.

CONCLUSION

Always remember that God will open a supernatural door of utterance for you if you will trust Him. God desires to promote His people into the ministry He has called them to. As you prepare and trust Him, doors of opportunity will open that only God could arrange.

6

Basic Needs for the Traveling Ministry

You can start with as little or as much office space and equipment as you want when you get started in the traveling ministry. In reality, you can start with very little office space or equipment since your "clientele" will not be visiting your office. In this lesson, I discuss some basic office, correspondence, and transportation items that a person may need to get started in the traveling ministry.

In the traveling ministry, you can approach purchasing ministry equipment differently than paying your expenses. A wise approach is to borrow money only for things that bring a return to you, such as a computer that helps you

Make an inventory list of items you already have that you can use for your traveling ministry.

_____

_____

_____

_____

_____

_____

_____

_____

_____

_____

_____

_____

_____

_____

_____

_____

design products or a vehicle that gets you to your meetings. Expenses (rent, light bill, etc.) will not bring a return to you, so you should avoid borrowing money to pay for them.

EQUIPMENT	EXPENSES
• Borrow money if necessary or lease to purchase • Equipment helps you accomplish your vision • Purchasing equipment is an investment	• Do not borrow money or lease to purchase • Expenses are the daily cost of your operation • Paying expenses is a liability

OFFICE NEEDS

- **An answering machine.** Be sure to check the features to ensure your needs are adequately met. The digital models seem to have some advantage over those that use a cassette tape to record messages. Select a machine with remote access which allows you to retrieve your messages by telephone while traveling to another location.
- **A caller ID unit hooked up to your telephone.** Often when people call while you are gone, they will not leave a message. However, with a caller ID unit you can know who has called you, and you can

call people back even though they didn't leave a message.

- **A typewriter or computer.** Choose the kind of equipment that allows you to handle your correspondence promptly and properly. Make sure that your choice of equipment is not outdated or unable to work with the latest technology.

- **An adding machine.** This is necessary to help you make accurate financial plans and transactions. Generally a desk model makes your work easier to do and gives less chance of making a mistake.

- **A desk and chair.** These are simple things, yet necessary to effectively study and do your administrative work. Use whatever you have available to start with. However, you may soon want to purchase an adequate desk and a comfortable chair to help you do your work more easily.

CORRESPONDENCE NEEDS

Establish an address by getting a Post Office Box. Your residence may change, but if you have a P. O. Box for your ministry, your mailing address will not necessarily change. This will help keep your printed material relevant and also help you avoid the cost of reprinting all your stationery letterhead, envelopes, and business cards.

Make a list of items you need to obtain for your traveling ministry.

_____

_____

_____

_____

_____

_____

_____

_____

_____

_____

_____

_____

_____

_____

_____

_____

_____

_____

_____

Personal Notes

_____

_____

_____

_____

_____

_____

_____

_____

_____

_____

_____

_____

_____

_____

_____

_____

_____

_____

You will need to purchase a stationery package which includes your ministry letterhead, envelopes, and business cards. This will give your ministry a look of professionalism and excellence. Your stationery becomes your representative wherever you can't be present, so it should be professionally designed in an excellent manner.

TIP: Photocopying or using your computer to print your ministry letterhead on high quality paper like Classic Linen or Classic Laid may be a cost-effective way to start. As soon as possible, you'll want to have a stationery package including letterhead, envelopes, and business cards.

TIP: When it comes to getting business cards printed, make sure the cards aren't cluttered with print, are easy to read, and have a professional appearance. Make sure your business cards pass the two-second test! The average person looks at a business card for only two seconds. For this reason, they will only remember the most dominant item on your business card — which should be your name. This way they may forget your ministry name, but they won't forget your name as easily.

You may want to keep a supply of small greeting cards with a scripture verse on the outside and room for a handwritten message on the inside. This can be used to as a way to express your thanks and appreciation.

These card packets can be found in most Christian bookstores.

Usually people like to receive personal notes from other people. Do not hesitate to write a handwritten note to someone thanking them for a meeting or a gift. The person who takes time to say "thank you" has prepared the way for future relationships and meetings.

TRANSPORTATION NEEDS

Using your faith is necessary for whatever transportation you use. Start your traveling ministry with what you have. However, faith is not a substitute for regular maintenance on your vehicle. Regular maintenance at home will cost less than emergency repairs on the road.

In ten years of traveling thousands of miles, I have never had a major breakdown while I was on the road. I had built a relationship with a garage that did regular maintenance on my vehicles. They saved me from several potential disasters on the road by spotting things that were wrong and fixing them while I was at home.

Tips concerning transportation in the traveling ministry:

1. Use whatever vehicle you have.
2. Always apply your faith toward it.
3. Pray over your vehicle and dedicate it to God's work.

Personal Notes

4. Do regular maintenance on your vehicle.

5. Obey the laws of the land as you travel.

6. Have prayer at the beginning of every trip, taking authority over the power of the devil and all evil forces, so they cannot come against you on your trip.

7. Trust God to get you home safely without any major trouble.

CONCLUSION

This lesson has shown you some items needed to get started. Establish the call, establish the time, use what you've got, and expect God to bring the increase!

Administrative Needs in
The Traveling Ministry

7

Banking Decisions

Choosing the correct bank and learning to work with your banker can literally save your day (and your ministry)! Do your best not to be ignorant about financial principles or what your bank can do to help you.

Some ministers do not realize the importance of having knowledge of financial principles and the banking industry. However, if you want to be successful in the traveling ministry, you need to be responsible in the areas of finances. You need to be able to balance the ministry's books, read and prepare a financial statement, and be

ISAIAH 48:17
Thus saith the Lord, thy Redeemer, the Holy One of Israel; I am the Lord thy God which teacheth thee to profit, which leadeth thee by the way that thou shouldest go.

Personal Notes

_____

_____

_____

_____

_____

_____

_____

_____

_____

_____

_____

_____

able to explain your financial dealings to your ministry board members.

CHOOSING A BANK

Different banks have different fees and policies. They are not all the same. When choosing a bank for your ministry, contact at least six different banks in your city or community. Ask what they have to offer, and get the following information:

1. Types of checking accounts and their fees.
2. Types of savings accounts, their requirements, and interest rates paid.
3. Availability of Visa, MasterCard, and other credit cards for your ministry.
4. Information to set up a credit card merchant's account (to accept credit card payment when selling books and tapes).
5. Types of loans and rates of interest available.

There may be a bank in your city or community that waives all fees for nonprofit organizations. Although you may still have to pay for your checks and checkbook, that is a great way to save money.

When you are choosing a bank, note the availability of bank personnel and their friendliness toward you. Those two things should be important factors in your decision whether to choose or not choose a particular bank.

Ask what kind of clientele the bank caters to. This helps you determine whether they even want ministries and nonprofit organizations as their clientele. It will also let you know if they can or will give you the service you need for your ministry.

DOING BUSINESS WITH A BANK

Opening up a ministry account is something you should endeavor to do when you have sufficient income to do so. It provides a way to accurately keep track of ministry income. It is best to leave a clear paper trail with the finances of your ministry, such as bank deposits, checks written for expenses, and receipts for expenses.

You should avoid doing your ministry business in cash because it leaves no paper trail to verify the legality of your ministry operation. If you are ever audited by the Internal Revenue Service (IRS), you will be glad you have a clear paper trail so that you can prove what you did or did not do with your finances.

You will need to set up a checking account so you can deposit your income and also pay your expenses. Most banks have a variety of options available for checking accounts, such as regular checking or interest-bearing checking. Checking accounts are a good way to keep a paper trail of how your ministry finances are disbursed.

Use savings accounts for keeping designated funds and money for specific purposes separate from the general fund in your checking account. A savings account may be used to provide for:

1. A piece of equipment
2. A missions trip
3. A benevolence fund

I have seen ministries that continually spend every penny that comes in. They make no attempt to save any money. Consequently they do not have the funds when they need it, nor do they have any reserve when a crisis comes. Ministries with no finances in reserve in a savings account only need a little crisis to upset their delicate financial condition.

The Bible instructs us to be prudent in our financial dealings. Saving money is not a lack of faith. Saving money is using wisdom to prepare properly for the days ahead. Saving money provides a margin or reserve so that when an emergency occurs or a special need arises, you are not faced with a major crisis or bankruptcy.

I have noticed that if ministries will put aside ten percent of all the money that comes in, they usually won't experience any significant lack, and they will have finances for special projects or opportunities when they arise.

Develop a relationship with a loan officer at your bank before you need a loan. Generally, loans are given only if you meet a certain criteria. However, if a loan officer knows you and your character, they may give you the loan you need anyway, based upon a combination of your character, their criteria, and the cash you have on hand.

However, if you do not have a relationship with your banker, they will only consider your current financial condition and whether or not you can meet their criteria. Having a relationship with your banker allows your personal character to be another factor when the bank is making a decision as to whether or not they will give you the money you need. So developing a relationship with your banker, or with a loan officer at your bank, when you do not really need to borrow any money may help you later on when you do need to borrow money.

Again, relationships are important, both within and without the Body of Christ. Friends will do things for each other that they would not do for anyone else. Learn to cultivate good relationships with people at your bank and also with other people who can give you sound financial advice.

While you need faith to move with God, you need wisdom in dealing with the world's systems — including the banking industry. Faith may get you the finances you need. However, you also need the wisdom of God so that you will know what to do with the money that comes in.

Personal Notes

JAMES 1:5
If any of you lack wisdom, let him ask of God, that giveth to all men liberally, and upbraideth not; and it shall be given him.

Some people use the wisdom of God in their finances, and their finances seem to multiply. They do not seem to have any significant financial lack or trouble. Other people can have the same amount of income, and because they do not use the wisdom of God, they never seem to have enough money.

CONCLUSION

You may want to consider going to special seminars in your area to learn how to deal wisely with finances. You may also want to take a basic accounting class, so if you have people working for you and handling your money, you can at least recognize if they were to handle your finances incorrectly.

Financial decisions are a part of the ministry. Your ministry can rise or fall based upon how you handle your money. The main issue is to not be ignorant and to continue to learn about financial management principles and how to apply them in your ministry.

8

Keeping Records Is Vital to Your Ministry

Keeping accurate records for your ministry is a must! Whether you keep records manually or on your computer, record-keeping is not something you can afford to neglect.

More and more ministries are keeping their records on computer. This enables them to easily summarize the information and produce accurate financial statements.

KEEP RECORDS FOR ACCURATE INFORMATION

Most companies have a time of inventory and evaluation, so they can know the current condition of the

PROVERBS 24:3,4 (TLB)

Any enterprise is built upon wise planning, becomes strong through common sense, and profits wonderfully by keeping abreast of the facts.

Personal Notes

company and also make realistic projections for the future. Just because ministries deal with the spiritual aspect of reaching people for Christ does not mean that ministries do not have to pay attention to the natural elements of business management.

- Records provide a means of evaluating your ministry.
- Records help you make sound and wise decisions.
- Records enable you to plan for ministry in the future.

FINANCIAL RECORDS

Here are some items you may need in order to keep accurate financial records. Financial records are necessary to satisfy the legal requirements of the IRS and are helpful to show to bankers when applying for a loan. If you are keeping your records on computer, you may not need all of these items.

- A receipt book is necessary to record all income and keep track of individual donors. Office supply stores have them for sale.
- A general ledger is necessary to record income and expenses. Ledgers and cash journal books are also available at your local office supply store. See the samples at the end of this lesson.

- A form showing the contributions of each individual to your ministry. IRS regulations demand nonprofit organizations to provide individual donors with a receipt of their giving. For this reason you may need a form similar to the sample at the end of this lesson.

A place to get a complete record-keeping system for your ministry is:

Consulting Development Service, Inc.

3336-E Heathstead Pl.

Charlotte, NC 28210-4378

704-553-1370

You may choose to keep all of your financial records on your computer. There are church management and financial software programs available to help you do this. Check with you local computer store or Christian bookstore. The following are some computer software programs to consider using for keeping records in your ministry:

Donors Plus

Justin Osteen & Associates, Inc.

3400 Montrose Ste. 900

Houston, TX 77006

713-522-4222

Power Church Plus

208 Ridgefield Drive.

Asheville, North Carolina 28806

800-486-1800

Personal Notes

Personal Notes

_____

_____

_____

_____

_____

_____

_____

_____

_____

_____

_____

_____

_____

_____

_____

_____

_____

_____

_____

_____

Membership Plus

Parsons Technology

One Parsons Drive

Hiawatha, IA 52233

800-223-6925

Automated Church Systems

P.O. Box 3990

Florence, SC 29502-3990

800-736-7425

RECORDS FOR MINISTRY EVENTS

A time management system can be used to schedule your day, week, month, or year. It can also provide a record of what transpired on a certain day or at a certain ministry event.

Noting ministry events enables you to plan more effectively for the future.

1. Include geographical location, type of ministry, and what kind of results were obtained.

2. This will help you with your goal setting for future ministry.

As your schedule becomes busier, a time management system is very important. It frees up your mind to think on other things and enables you to keep your appointments.

Learning to manage our time is vital to our success in ministry. Whether we manage our time or not, life keeps on going. Lou Erickson said, "Life is like a taxi. The meter just keeps a-ticking whether you are getting somewhere or just standing still." In order to get the most accomplished that you can, put yourself on some kind of time-management system.

Some recommended time-management systems include:

Day-Timers, Inc.
One Day-Timer Plaza
Allenton, PA 18195-1551
1-800-225-5005
Day Runner, Inc.
(Available in most department stores.)

Tempus (A ministry-oriented system.)
8210 E. 71st St. Ste 139
Tulsa, OK 74133
1-800-728-6666

CONCLUSION

There are various kinds of record-keeping systems. Choose a system that will work for you, produce the information you need, and keep you abreast of the facts.

Some points to remember in successful record-keeping are:

- Be consistent — stick with the system you decide to use.

Personal Notes

Personal Notes

- Be disciplined — choose a regular time to get it done.

Remember the value of keeping accurate records is that it may provide the proof you need at a later date to verify certain actions or events.

SAMPLE OF A GENERAL LEDGER

GENERAL LEDGER

SHEET #_____

ACCOUNT NAME_____ ACCOUNT #_____

DATE	DESCRIPTION	DEBIT	CREDITS	BALANCE	
				DEBITS	CREDITS

SAMPLE OF AN INDIVIDUAL'S
CONTRIBUTION LEDGER

NAME	
ADDRESS	
CITY	ST
ZIP	FILE #

_____QUARTER   _____YEAR

DATE	GIFTS	MISSIONS	BUILDING FUND	OFFERINGS	OTHER
TOTAL					

TOTAL CONTRIBUTIONS   _____QUARTER [   ]

9

Legal Concerns for Traveling Ministers

A traveling ministry must consider a number of things that affect it legally. For example, a traveling ministry should be prepared for the legal requirements of the following:

1. Incorporation
2. Tax-exempt status with the IRS and compliance issues
3. Tax requirements, such as sales and property taxes, where not exempt in the States
4. Donor record-keeping and reporting
5. Business operational issues

MATTHEW 22:21

...Render therefore unto Caesar the things which are Caesar's; and unto God the things that are God's.

Personal Notes

_____

_____

_____

_____

_____

_____

_____

_____

_____

_____

_____

_____

_____

_____

_____

_____

6. Minister's salary, housing allowances, and ordination or licensing
7. Employment law issues, such as discrimination, labor/wage and hour issues, sexual harassment, hiring and firing issues, worker's compensation and unemployment taxes, and pension laws
8. Record-keeping requirements of various state and federal agencies
9. Ministerial misconduct policies
10. Liability issues

There are also legal issues affecting each licensed or ordained minister who is part of the traveling ministry. These issues include, for example, various income tax regulations, Social Security taxes, legal liability, state requirements to perform marriages, visit penal institutions, report child abuse, and the like. Here we will touch on general issues of incorporation and obtaining tax-exempt status.

OBTAINING NONPROFIT STATUS

The first consideration is whether you wish for contributors to your ministry to be able to deduct their donations from their taxes. If so, your ministry must file an application for exemption with the Internal Revenue Service and be approved as a tax-exempt organization. This exemption both qualifies your ministry as exempt from paying federal income taxes on income received by the ministry and also qualifies donations received for charitable deductions by the donors. The IRS publishes a listing (Publication 78) of exempt organizations. Many donors are reluctant to donate to an organization not listed.

A traveling ministry will normally be treated differently under the Internal Revenue Code (IRC) than a church. While both are exempt from paying taxes under IRC § 501(c)(3), and both may receive donations which are deductible to the donor under IRC § 170, the rules are different for a traveling ministry both for obtaining and keeping tax-exempt status with the IRS.

IRC § 508 permits group exemption. This allows a church or ministry to closely affiliate with an exempt church and come under the "umbrella" of the exempt church. So a traveling ministry has the choice of affiliating with a church which has a group exemption by complying with the IRS and that church's requirements or obtaining exempt status for itself. Several church organizations have IRS group exemptions and will accept traveling ministries. They should have a group exemption number from the IRS.

Your other option is to seek tax-exempt status for your ministry. In the last ten years, the process of obtaining exempt status has become more difficult. Abuses have caused a stricter scrutiny of ministries seeking tax-exempt status. It has also become more expensive. However, it is more expensive to try to correct a problem than to do it right in the first place. You should contact an attorney

Personal Notes

who is knowledgeable in the area of nonprofit religious organizations for assistance.

Tax laws are complex in this country. The laws governing nonprofit exempt organizations and ministers can be especially frustrating. It is important to retain an attorney knowledgeable in obtaining tax-exempt status to help you through the process of getting your exemption.

INCORPORATION

Usually a traveling ministry should incorporate in a state of its choice. Incorporation creates a legal entity which provides some protection should you be sued. This can be done very simply, but this is not always wise. The danger of the easy path is that often the incorporating documents do not comply with IRS requirements for exempt status.

Requirements vary from state to state as to the contents of articles and bylaws or other documents forming a nonprofit or religious corporation. Several attorneys specialize in religious exempt organizations and can incorporate you in any of the fifty states.

EXAMPLE:

Winters, King, & Associates, Inc.

2448 E. 81st St., Ste. 5900

Tulsa, OK 74137-4259

918-494-6868

Fax: 918-491-6297

In choosing your Board of Trustees or Directors you will have to have the minimum number required by the state laws where you are incorporated. Be careful whom you choose to serve on your Board of Trustees or Directors. Investigate each person before you put him or her on your Board of Trustees of Directors. Make sure all member candidates:

1. Are honest and capable in business dealings.
2. Have a good report in their local church.
3. Know you and support your ministry.
4. Are in agreement with the vision and purpose of your ministry.

In addition to incorporation, the ministry should register any trade names, trademarks, copyrights, and register with state departments as well as obtain a federal employer identification number (E.I.N.) — the corporate version of a personal social security number. If you own or purchase real estate property, and if local law permits, you may be able to obtain exemption from property taxes. Your attorney and/or certified public accountant (CPA) can help you with this.

Once incorporated, your Board of Trustees or Directors should meet at least once a year to take care of corporate business. The board must authorize whoever signs contracts and commits the ministry to major purchases or sales of assets. You should be careful to keep

Personal Notes

corporate minutes on board approval for every major transaction or decision authorizing the corporation to act.

Keeping records of both financial and legal documents is critical. Records of donations — whether money or property — must be kept. Contracts and deeds and other documents of title should be kept in an organized manner and in a safe place. Files on all employees should be maintained as in any business. The ministry should not reimburse a traveling staff member without receipts and good records of mileage and other expenses. Otherwise, the reimbursement would be treated as income.

TAXES — STATE AND FEDERAL

As mentioned previously, there are a plethora of state and federal tax laws relating to nonprofit or religious organizations and to licensed or ordained ministers. Along with retaining a lawyer, it is also recommended that you retain a certified public accountant knowledgeable in tax-exempt organizations to handle the accounting and tax filings for both your ministry and the personal taxes of ordained or licensed ministers in your organization. It is also wise to let your attorney and CPA work together where needed.

Here are two organizations that are available to help with tax returns:

Sandra Siegfried, CPA

Stanfield & O'Dell

3211 S. Lakewood

Tulsa, OK 74135

918-628-0500

Terry Mosley, CPA

8252 S. Harvard, #155

Tulsa, OK 74137

918-491-6063

Other legal organizations include:

Christian Ministry Resources

P.O. Box 2301

Matthews, NC 28106

704-841-8066

CONCLUSION

Remember these things:

1. Know the limits of your competency and get wise counsel beyond that.
2. Hire a professional knowledgeable in the areas in which you need help.
3. Don't be "pound foolish and penny wise." In other words, pay a professional to start you out right and keep you on track. The cost of not doing so can be very great.

Personal Notes

4. God has appointed governing authorities for our good. The IRS and other agencies are not to be feared when we are determined to act righteously. God promised to surround us with favor as a shield (Ps 5:12)!

Note: This lesson was contributed by M. Jean Holmes, attorney with Winters, King, and Associates, Inc. This firm represents numerous churches and ministries all over the United States, as well as people on the mission field. This firm is located at 2448 E. 81st St. #5900, Tulsa, OK 74137, and can be reached at (918) 494-6868.

10

Developing Your Personal Action Plan

God has instructed us to write down the vision, instructions, or direction that we receive from Him. The revelation of God's will may contain very specific assignments that He wants you to accomplish. In the case of Moses, God gave him very detailed instructions as to how to build the Tabernacle.

God may share details concerning His will for your life and ministry more at certain times than at other times. Learn to write down whatever God reveals to you so that you can get ready to do it. This involves develop-

HABAKKUK 2:2,3
And the Lord answered me, and said, Write the vision, and make it plain upon tables, that he may run that readeth it.
For the vision is yet for an appointed time, but at the end it shall speak, and not lie: though it tarry, wait for it; because it will surely come, it will not tarry.

Personal Notes

_____

_____

_____

_____

_____

_____

_____

_____

_____

_____

ing a corresponding action plan to achieve what God has said.

Developing your own action plan involves several things:

1. Writing a Mission Statement.
2. Writing goals to achieve your Mission Statement.
3. Evaluating both spiritual and natural conditions to meet the above two items.

DEVELOPING YOUR MISSION STATEMENT

- Make it specific. Avoid being too vague or trying to say too much.
- Make it scriptural. God will not bless anything else.
- Make it brief — no more than three paragraphs long.
- Make it in agreement with the call of God on your life.
- Include the purpose for your traveling ministry.
- Include the values you adhere to.

EXAMPLE: Paul's mission statement was in agreement with the call of God upon his life. Compare Acts 26:16-19 (God's call) with Romans 1:14-17 (Paul's mission statement).

ACTS 26:16-19

But rise, and stand upon thy feet: for I have appeared unto thee for this purpose, to make thee a minister and a witness both of these things which thou hast seen, and of those things in the which I will appear unto thee;

Delivering thee from the people, and from the Gentiles, unto whom now I send thee,

To open their eyes, and to turn them from darkness to light, and from the power of Satan unto God, that they may receive forgiveness of sins, and inheritance among them which are sanctified by faith that is in me.

Whereupon, O king Agrippa, I was not disobedient unto the heavenly vision.

ROMANS 1:14-17

I am debtor both to the Greeks, and to the Barbarians; both to the wise, and to the unwise.

So, as much as in me is, I am ready to preach the gospel to you that are at Rome also.

For I am not ashamed of the gospel of Christ: for it is the power of God unto salvation to every one that believeth; to the Jew first, and also to the Greek.

For therein is the righteousness of God revealed from faith to faith: as it is written, The just shall live by faith.

Consider your calling, purpose, values, and objectives when developing your mission statement. These all have to be in agreement.

Personal Notes

Personal Notes

_____

_____

_____

_____

_____

_____

_____

_____

_____

_____

_____

_____

_____

_____

_____

_____

_____

Write down the purpose for your traveling ministry.

_____

_____

_____

_____

_____

_____

_____

What scriptures correspond with your purpose?

_____

_____

_____

_____

_____

_____

_____

_____

_____

Write down the values that you adhere to — both as a person and as a minister.

_____

_____

_____

_____

_____

_____

_____

What scriptures correspond with your personal and ministerial values?

_____

_____

_____

_____

_____

_____

_____

_____

Personal Notes

Personal Notes

_____

_____

_____

_____

_____

_____

_____

_____

_____

_____

_____

_____

_____

_____

_____

_____

_____

_____

_____

_____

_____

_____

Write down the objective, or end result, you want to achieve through your traveling ministry.

_____

_____

_____

_____

_____

_____

_____

Corresponding scriptures:

_____

_____

_____

_____

_____

_____

_____

_____

_____

_____

Now you have a broad statement of the mission God has given to you. Next you need to break the mission down into steps that you can negotiate easily.

DEVELOPING YOUR GOALS

Goals are steps to accomplishing your mission. As you grow in the knowledge of God and His Word, you will know more and more the steps that God wants you to take and the corresponding goals to set.

Goals should be written down, be measurable, and have a time limit.

Seven questions to ask when setting a goal*:

1. What is the goal?
2. When is the goal to be done?
3. What obstacles need to be removed to achieve the goal?
4. Who are the people and organizations I need in order to accomplish the goal?
5. What skills do I need in order to develop and complete my goal?
6. What is my plan of action to achieve the goal?
7. What are the rewards of this goal?

* Adapted from Zig Ziglar's "Seven Steps in Goal Setting"

PSALM 37:23
The steps of a good man are ordered of the Lord, and he delighteth in his way.

Personal Notes

_____

_____

_____

_____

_____

_____

_____

_____

_____

_____

_____

_____

_____

_____

_____

_____

Personal Notes

_____

_____

_____

_____

_____

_____

_____

_____

_____

_____

_____

_____

_____

_____

_____

_____

_____

_____

_____

1 CORINTHIANS 2:16
For who hath known the mind of the Lord, that he may instruct him? But we have the mind of Christ.

WRITING DOWN YOUR GOALS

Write down sixty-day goals that will help you accomplish your mission statement. Ask yourself the seven previous questions about each goal to make sure what you are trying to attain is really something you want.

1. _____

_____

2. _____

_____

3. _____

_____

4. _____

_____

5. _____

_____

6. _____

_____

7. _____

_____

8. _____

_____

Write down one-year goals that will help you accomplish your mission statement. Again, ask yourself the seven previously-listed questions to make sure each goal is something you truly want.

1. _____

2. _____

3. _____

4. _____

5. _____

6. _____

7. _____

Write down five-year goals that will help you accomplish your mission statement. Again, ask yourself the seven questions listed to make sure each goal is really something you want.

1. _____

2. _____

3. _____

4. _____

5. _____

6. _____

7. _____

Personal Notes

Personal Notes

Keep these goals in a place where you can review them at regular intervals to make sure you are on course. Remember, these goals should be steps in accomplishing your mission statement.

Your goals will probably have to be updated and "fine-tuned" as you go along. Don't be concerned if you still don't know much about what God wants you to do. But write down what you do know, and then make sure you follow through to get it done.

Once you have a plan, it is up to you to work it. Many are waiting for perfect circumstances or something they don't have before they start. Get started with what you have — the world is waiting for you, and so is God.

Remember what Rupert Hughs said: "The determined soul will do more with a rusty monkey wrench than a loafer will with all the tools in a mechanic's shop."

CONCLUSION

Now we have written down our mission statement and set our goals. The next two pages are designed to help you evaluate your spiritual, material, and physical condition to determine what you have and what you still need in order to get started in the traveling ministry.

ESTABLISHING YOUR TRAVELING
MINISTRY WORKSHEET

What type of traveling ministry are you going to have?

☐ Teaching   ☐ Musician

☐ Missionary   ☐ Evangelist

☐ Exhorter   ☐ Other (list)

_____

Who would you seek counsel from before you start the traveling ministry?

☐ Pastor   ☐ Your spouse

☐ Close friends/associates   ☐ Banker

☐ Employer   ☐ Other (list)

_____

Write down three role models you look to for spiritual counsel or as an example in establishing your traveling ministry.

1. _____

2. _____

3. _____

Write down the first thing you need to do to get started in the traveling ministry.

Spiritually _____

_____

Materially _____

_____

List some other things that you need to do to help you accomplish your purpose in ministry.

Spiritually

1. _____

2. _____

3. _____

4. _____

5. _____

Materially

1. _____

2. _____

3. _____

4. _____

5. _____

Administrative/Marketing

1. _____

2. _____

3. _____

4. _____

5. _____

List some practical day-to-day steps you need to take to implement the things you just listed.

1. _____

_____

2. _____

_____

3. _____

_____

4. _____

_____

5. _____

_____

What kind of people or professional services do you need to help you with the traveling ministry?

☐ Administrator/bookkeeper   ☐ Secretary

☐ Mechanical/utility person   ☐ Music personnel

☐ Marketing person   ☐ Other (list below)

1. _____

2. _____

3. _____

4. _____

5. _____

6. _____

List what kind of equipment you need in order to function in the traveling ministry. Decide what you need just to get started and then what you need to accomplish your mission statement.

1._____

2._____

3._____

4._____

5._____

6._____

How much money do you need to get started in the traveling ministry? (Estimate for one year)

☐ $5,000 - $10,000   ☐ $10,000 - $20,000

☐ $20,000 - $_____

Where do you plan to get the money for the first year?

☐ Personal money   ☐ Offerings/gifts

☐ Fund-raising events   ☐ Partners

☐ Loans   ☐ Other (list below)

1._____

2._____

3._____

How much planning time will you need before your traveling ministry begins?

☐ 1 month   ☐ 6 months   ☐ 1 year

☐ Other (list)_____

What contacts, organizations, and support will you need to help you in the traveling ministry?

☐ Ministerial organizations (list below)

☐ Local church support   ☐ Prayer group

☐ Local business support   ☐ Pastoral contacts

☐ Other (list below)

1. _____

2. _____

3. _____

List some things you hope to accomplish in one year.

1. _____

_____

2. _____

_____

3. _____

_____

4. _____

_____

5. _____

_____

6. _____

_____

List some things you hope to accomplish in five years.

1. _____

_____

2. _____

_____

3. _____

_____

4. _____

_____

5. _____

_____

6. _____

_____

Name one or more projects that you know God wants you to accomplish or that you desire to do.

1. _____

_____

2. _____

_____

3. _____

_____

4. _____

_____

5. _____

_____

6. _____

_____

Write a paragraph describing the kind of traveling ministry you are attempting to establish.

_____

_____

_____

_____

_____

_____

_____

_____

_____

_____

_____

Personal Notes

_____

_____

_____

_____

_____

_____

_____

_____

_____

_____

_____

_____

_____

_____

_____

_____

_____

_____

_____

_____

CONCLUSION

Keep this book with you so you can refer to it periodically. You may have to make copies of this lesson so you can update it as you go along. This represents the vision for your ministry. It is up to you to accomplish the vision with God's wisdom, guidance, and power. God bless you — go for it!

Scheduling Meetings in Churches

Scheduling Meetings in Churches
PART ONE

Scheduling meetings in churches without being pushy and while keeping your motives right is an art that has to be learned if you are going to be successful in the traveling ministry. This section is meant to give some general guidelines for traveling ministries.

You must seek the Lord as to what specific plan of action He would have you to take. Ask God to reveal a strategy that will cause you to be successful. Next, be willing to live by the strategy that God gives you. Don't compare yourself with other traveling ministries.

1 THESSALONIANS 5:12
And we beseech you, brethren, to know them which labour among you, and are over you in the Lord, and admonish you.

Personal Notes

_____

_____

_____

_____

_____

_____

_____

_____

_____

_____

_____

_____

_____

_____

_____

_____

WHERE DO YOU START?

Who do you know in the ministry? Who you know can determine where you start in the traveling ministry.

Start with pastors and churches that you know and have a relationship with. You will probably obtain more meetings from friends and relatives than from any other source. You may want to consider writing an Introductory Letter about your ministry and sending it to everyone you know.

Some traveling ministers do "cold calling," which means they contact people they don't know personally. I have not found this method to be very successful, simply because we live in a day when accountability is a concern to many people. The Scriptures tell us to know those who labor among us.

RELATIONSHIPS AND REFERRALS

In my traveling ministry I have worked mostly through relationships and referrals. Relationships develop into meetings. If the only time you talk to pastors is when you need a meeting, that meeting source may dry up. Take an interest in the pastor's life, family, and ministry even at times when you are not scheduling a meeting with them.

Relationships with other ministers can be built by going to ministers' conferences or regional ministers' meetings and getting acquainted with the ministers in attendance. You will "click" with some and not with others. Build a relationship with those it seems God has put you together with.

Don't be pushy at ministers' meetings by presenting your brochure to every pastor there. They are there to relax, refire, and learn. If a minister asks about your ministry, be ready to give him a brochure. If he doesn't ask, talk about his ministry.

Go to a ministers' meeting with the idea of giving to other ministers. That will make you stand out in the crowd and cause others to take notice of you. I have often taken other ministers out to lunch just to develop a relationship with them. Not once during the course of the meal did I ask for a meeting. Sometimes months later, a pastor I took to lunch would call me and schedule a meeting.

When developing relationships with pastors, remember that the relationship is more important than getting a meeting. Even if a pastor never invites you to minister in his church, the relationship is valuable. Don't go have lunch with a pastor just to get a meeting. Pastors will feel that, and you may get a meeting from them, but the relationship will never be what it could have been.

Referrals can work well to get meetings for you. If a pastor indicates that he was blessed by your ministry, perhaps he would be willing to refer you to his pastoral friends and acquaintances. Approach the pastor carefully about this. Some pastors do not want to do this even if

Personal Notes

Personal Notes

they like your ministry. Referrals can help to warm up those "cold calls" that you make to pastors by providing a mutual acquaintance for both of you.

CONCLUSION

Remember, if God called you into the traveling ministry, He will open the doors of opportunity for you. God will create a place for your gift to manifest. Proverbs 18:16 will help you keep things in proper perspective.

PROVERBS 18:16
A man's gift maketh room for him, and bringeth him before great men.

12

Scheduling Meetings in Churches
PART TWO

The way you make initial contact with a pastor is very important. Initial contact creates "first impressions." Usually within the first five minutes of contact the pastor will decide whether or not he will invite you to his church.

INITIAL CONTACT IN PERSON

Dress well when contacting a pastor in person. Let your dress reflect the mission you want to accomplish. It is better to be a little over-dressed than to not be dressed well enough.

Personal Notes

Manners, etiquette, and protocol are very important. Taking the time to learn proper manners and etiquette can cause you to receive invitations to preach that others don't get.

Pastors take notice when traveling ministers who show up at their church are not dressed neatly or don't conduct themselves in an excellent manner.

Using good business sense is another way to make a good impression upon a pastor. With your traveling schedule, the pastor may not have an opportunity to see you conduct yourself in a business situation. But whenever you are around the pastor or the people, be sure to show good business sense.

Things to consider when making initial contact in person are:

1. Be considerate of the pastor's views and needs. Listen more than you talk. Talk about the pastor's concerns.

2. Be generous to the pastor. Pay for lunch or give them a gift or a tape that will bless them. Most traveling ministers don't do this, but it's a great way to help the pastor remember you.

3. Be appreciative of what the pastor and the church do for you. Be sure to send a thank-you note to them.

4. Be honest about your ministry. Honesty will get you farther than big stories or big names will.

5. Be specific about your ministry. Share the areas your ministry is effective in. Don't try to be and do everything.

INITIAL CONTACT BY MAIL

There is a lot of unsolicited direct mail sent out in America. All of it is vying for someone's attention. I have noticed that in the midst of all the unsolicited mail I get, only two kinds really catch my eye — the really bad material and the very good material. Of course, we don't want our ministry associated with the really bad material.

Your advertising material about your traveling ministry represents you. Recipients form their opinion of your ministry by the material you send to them. Therefore, you want your advertising material to be as excellent as possible.

How much should you spend for advertising materials, such as brochures, business cards, and stationery? In making your decision, consider both "price" and "cost." "Price" is what you pay for the material, printing, etc. "Cost" is when your material creates a negative impact and costs you a meeting. "Cost" can last a lifetime, while "price" is a one-time fee. Saving on "price" may raise your "cost."

TIP: Figure your budget for advertising and contact material per year according to what you would expect your offering to be in one meeting. If

Personal Notes

Personal Notes

your average offering for one meeting is $500, then spend approximately $500 for advertising material that year.

Contact material to send in the mail can include the following:

1. A Letter of Introduction letting the pastor know about you and when you are planning to be in his area
2. A brochure telling about your ministry
3. A business card
4. A Letter of Recommendation from a pastor who knows you

A Letter of Introduction sent out to pastors can be very effective. On one sheet of your letterhead, tell about you and your ministry and supply an address and telephone number by which you can be contacted. (See the sample Letters of Introduction on page 89 and 90).

A Letter of Recommendation from a pastor who is familiar with your ministry may accompany your Letter of Introduction. Pastors are concerned about having only reputable traveling ministers come to their church to speak. A Letter of Recommendation shows accountability and provides the pastor with a way of evaluating your ministry.

A Ministry Packet, which can include the following items, may be sent to pastors who are interested in receiving more information about your ministry.

1. **A cover letter.** A letter explaining why you're sending the Ministry Packet should be included with the ministry literature.

2. **A ministry fact sheet.** A fact sheet is like a menu at a restaurant — it shows what you have to offer. In it you may state the type of ministering you do (Singles Retreats, Marriage Enrichment, Revivals, Healing Crusades, Faith/Prosperity Seminars, etc.), the history of your ministry, and facts and statistics of things accomplished in your ministry.

3. **Letters of recommendation** from ministers who know you or from the pastors of churches where you ministered.

4. **A press release** that the church can use to advertise the meetings.

5. **An audiotape** of a short message that you have shared.

INITIAL CONTACT BY TELEPHONE

Contacting by telephone will cause an immediate good or bad impression. If talking on the telephone isn't your strong point, perhaps you should consider some other way of contacting pastors. Another alternative is to have someone else make the telephone calls for you, although pastors are usually not impressed by this.

Personal Notes

_____

_____

_____

_____

_____

_____

_____

_____

_____

_____

_____

COLOSSIANS 4:2-4
Continue in prayer, and watch in the same with thanksgiving;
Withal praying also for us, that God would open unto us a door of utterance, to speak the mystery of Christ, for which I am also in bonds:
That I may make it manifest, as I ought to speak.

Using the telephone is possibly the least desirable or effective way to contact pastors initially. The pastor will know more about you and be able to make a better judgment if you contact them in person or by mail.

The telephone can be used successfully if:

1. You are acquainted with the pastor or have already established a relationship with the pastor.
2. You have already preached in the pastor's church before.

The telephone is a good follow-up tool, after having made initial contact by mail or in person. It is good business sense to follow up with a telephone call after mailing a brochure to the pastor or after contacting them in person.

Bad telephone techniques can turn a person off and create a negative image for your ministry. So if talking on the telephone is not something you know how to do very well, reading a book on telemarketing techniques may help you. They are usually available at your local public library.

CONCLUSION

Whether you contact a pastor in person, by mail, or by telephone, the first impression you make is often a lasting one. Therefore, excellence is necessary in this area — as in everything you do. And remember, practice makes perfect!

SAMPLE LETTER OF INTRODUCTION #1

(Date)

Dear Pastor_____(Name)_____,

I am writing this letter to introduce you to Marvin Yoder Ministries.

I grew up in the Old Order Amish Church, driving a horse and buggy and having no radio or television in my home. It is an exciting story how God made Himself known to me when I was a ten-year-old Amish boy and started me on the path He ordained for my life.

As a teenager I ran away from home and became a pool hustler, living in bars and pool halls. But God made Himself real to me once again, saving me, delivering me, and healing me of many physical ailments.

My wife, Leah, who is also from the Old Order Amish Church, and I have three daughters, Christina Anne, Nichole Joy, and Audrey Danielle.

In obedience to God's call to the ministry I attended Rhema Bible Training Center in Broken Arrow, Oklahoma. Since graduating in 1984, I have pastored several churches in Kansas and Illinois.

Presently we are traveling in the Body of Christ teaching the Word of God with special emphasis on the Holy Spirit. Often God demonstrates His power and the gifts of the Spirit manifest in our meetings. I have shared in many denominations, including Assembly of God, Brethren, Baptist, Charismatic, Mennonite, Methodist, Nazarene, and Word of Faith Churches.

We believe you'll be blessed by the practical and often humorous preaching of the Word of God!

To schedule a meeting with us in your area, please contact:

Marvin Yoder Ministries
P.O. Box 168
Stonington, IL 62567
217-325-3637

I have also enclosed a brochure telling about our ministry. Thank you for taking time to read my material. I will look forward to speaking with you in the near future.

Sincerely,

Marvin Yoder

Marvin Yoder

Enclosures

SAMPLE LETTER OF INTRODUCTION #2

NICK WHITE

Dear Pastor_____(Name)_____ ,

I am writing to introduce to you Nick White Ministries. I have enclosed a brochure concerning myself and ministry for your information and review. I will also be glad to send you a tape of one of my services or a list of references if you so desire. You are welcome and invited to contact the Rhema Ministerial Association International offices at (918) 258-1588, extension 2312, and to contact the references listed concerning myself and my ministry.

I am planning to be in your area (see dates below) and would welcome the opportunity to minister for you and your congregation. I will contact you as soon as possible to discuss this possibility with you. If these dates do not fit your schedule at this time but you would be interested in another date, we can discuss that when I call.

I want to thank you for your time and consideration and will be looking forward to speaking with you in the near future.

Sincerely in Christ's Service,

Nick White

Enclosures

DATES IN YOUR AREA: _____

13

Scheduling Meetings in Churches

PART THREE

Often pastors begin planning for their upcoming year in October or November, and they may start scheduling meetings during these months. The traveling minister needs to be aware of a pastor's schedule so he can be available to help him. The fall is generally a good time to contact pastors to schedule meetings for the next year.

Have what you want to say written out in front of you. This can help you to stay focused on your objective.

If possible, work your schedule six months to a year ahead of time. For example, in November or December of this year, schedule meetings for April through December

Personal Notes

of next year. Pastors are more flexible if you contact them far enough in advance.

Give the pastor a date when you will be in his area. Also have an alternate date ready in case the first date doesn't work in the pastor's schedule. Once you have your first meetings in a particular area, other pastors may schedule you in their churches too. This allows various churches in the same area to share the expenses of hosting a traveling minister.

Here is one method of contacting pastors to schedule a meeting in their church. This method makes contact with the pastor five times.

1. Call first to see if the pastor would be interested in receiving an Introductory Letter of your ministry.
2. Next, send the Introductory Letter of your ministry.
3. Then follow up with a phone call to the pastor 7-10 days later to ask:
   - If he has received your letter.
   - If he wants to receive a Ministry Packet with additional information that you have available.
   - When he is scheduling meetings for next year, and if you can call him then.
4. Next, send your Ministry Packet to the pastor.
5. Then, follow up with a phone call to make sure the pastor received your Ministry Packet.

6. Finally, call back when the pastor said he is scheduling meetings to ask him to schedule you for a meeting.

Be a person of your word, sending your material in a timely manner when it's requested.

When you call the pastor to ask for a meeting, you might begin by saying, "I'm going to be in your area on (give a date when and also have a second date available)." If the pastor tells you he can't have you on those dates, respond, "No problem, when are you scheduling for next year?" When he tells you, ask him, "Is it all right for me to call you then to arrange a meeting for next year?"

Here is a list of things to talk about with the pastor when scheduling meetings in his church:

☐ The dates you will be in his area.

☐ Ask the question: "Is there a possibility of ministering in your church on (such-and-such) date?"

☐ Give information and facts about your ministry and recent events.

☐ Ask about the pastor and his church. Find out if your ministry is compatible with what is happening in his church right now.

☐ Gain a clear understanding of accommodations and financial arrangements.

☐ If you have books and tapes, ask the pastor if it is acceptable to set up a table for them.

Personal Notes

Personal Notes

☐ State how many people will be with you, if any.

☐ State the arrival and departure dates so the pastor knows how many nights' accommodation you will need.

☐ Discuss what promotional material you may need to send to the pastor to help promote the meetings in their church.

☐ State that you will send a letter of confirmation covering the details that were discussed.

It is a good idea to send a follow-up package to churches where you have scheduled meetings. That package may include a letter of confirmation, which should be sent in a timely manner — usually within one to two weeks following the initial contact with the pastor. In the letter you should cover the details that you discussed. This eliminates potential misunderstandings, and the pastor will know what to expect from you. (See the sample Letter of Confirmation on page 99.)

Any promotional material for your ministry that you have should also be included in the follow-up package. Offering promotional material shows you really want to help the pastor with his church rather than merely have another meeting. Some relatively inexpensive promotional materials you may offer include:

1. A black and white photo (approximately 2" x 3")

2. A sample press release (See the sample included on page 100.)

3. Handouts (5 1/2" x 8 1/2") that have ministry and meeting information to give the church members. This size fits inside most church bulletins. (See the sample on page 101.)

4. Posters (11" x 17") work well to promote the meetings to the public. Using a glossy paper with reflex blue ink done in a "printer's run" is very cost effective.

After sending the follow-up package, a telephone call to the pastor approximately one to three weeks ahead of the meeting dates is a good way to ensure that everything is still according to schedule.

KEEP A RECORD OF CHURCHES YOU CONTACT

Keeping records of when you contact pastors and churches is very important. This allows you to have the information of a particular church at hand when you contact each one.

Organization determines success and eliminates mistakes. Get a time management tool such as a Day-Timer schedule and calendar. Always carry your calendar and your business cards with you whenever you go.

Develop a Contact File of churches that contains information about them. This allows you to be more

Personal Notes

personable with each pastor. You can use 3x5 cards or a sheet like the sample on page 102. The following is vital information to include on your contact sheet:

1. Church name, address, phone number, and secretary's name.

2. The pastor's, his wife's, and their children's names; their birthdays, anniversaries, etc.

3. Log all contacts with the pastor/church and reason for it.

Develop a "tickler file" — an expandable file segmented by months.

Log all contact information that you need on a Contact File Card. If you are going to call the pastor back at a certain time, file that card in the appropriate month, so you can make sure you call that pastor at the right time.

MAKING FINANCIAL ARRANGEMENTS

You may bring the subject of finances up by asking the pastor, "What is your policy concerning guest speakers and offerings?" After they respond, you may state, "Most churches receive a love offering for me and take care of my food and lodging while I'm there, but I am open to whatever you are able to do." Be aware that some churches will give you a love offering and others will give you an honorarium.

Other questions to think about include:

- Who takes care of your traveling expenses? Do you take care of it, or does the church pay for it?
- If the church pays expenses, is the cost taken out of the offering or not? (TIP: Be conservative in your spending — most of the time you won't know for sure about the church's financial procedure until after the meetings.)
- Is expense money advanced or reimbursed?
- Are receipts required for reimbursement?
- Are only the expenses of the traveling minister taken care of, or will the church take care of his traveling companions?

NECESSARY FOLLOW-UP AFTER CONDUCTING MEETINGS IN CHURCHES

What you do after having your meetings will greatly determine whether you get invited back.

Send a letter of thanks — mention any specific or special things they did for you while you were there, such as meals, accommodations, fruit baskets, gifts, etc. Remember you are building relationships. (See the sample letter of thanks on page 103.)

Follow up everything in writing with a phone call, and confirm every phone call in writing. This lets the pastor

Personal Notes

Personal Notes

know you care about what happens in his church after you are there. Consistent follow-up makes the difference.

CONCLUSION

Do what you can to be a blessing to pastors and their churches. Treat them like you want to be treated. God will honor you and open doors of utterance for you.

SAMPLE LETTER OF MEETING CONFIRMATION

(Date)

Pastor _____(First and last names)_____
(Name of Church)
(Address)
(City, State & Zip)

Dear Pastor _____(Last name)_____,

Greetings in the Name of our Lord Jesus Christ!

To confirm the dates we had scheduled for me to be at your church, I have written down _____,20____ for both the A.M. and P.M. services. I will be arriving on Saturday, _____, 20____, at approximately 5 P.M. I will be traveling by myself. Please let me know if this is different than what we had discussed. I will contact you shortly before the dates that I am to be at your church.

I have also included 100 bulletin inserts, 6 posters, 1 press release sample, and 1 photo for you to use to promote the meetings in your church.

Thank you for allowing me to come to your church. If we can be of further assistance, please contact me at 217-325-3637. God bless you richly as you minister in His anointing.

Times of refreshing,

Marvin Yoder

Marvin Yoder
P.S. If possible, we would like a table for books and tapes.

SAMPLE PRESS RELEASE

PRESS RELEASE

(Date written)   Contact: (Name of Person)
For immediate release   (Phone Number)

WORD OF LIFE SEMINAR

(Church Name) announces Word of Life Seminars will be conducted on (date, time, and location) with guest minister Marvin Yoder.

Marvin Yoder grew up in the Old Order Amish Church, driving a horse and buggy and having no car, radio, or television in his home. It is an exciting story how God made Himself known to a 10-year-old Amish boy and caused him to travel the path He ordained for his life.

Marvin is a graduate of Rhema Bible Training Center in Broken Arrow, Oklahoma. Since graduating from Rhema, Marvin has pastored several churches in Kansas and Illinois. Presently Marvin conducts Word of Life Seminars.

Word of Life Seminars are designed to build up and refresh the Body of Christ. In these meetings you will receive knowledge for successful Christian living, be equipped to accomplish your God-given assignment, and be refreshed and refired for effective ministry.

(Include all church information such as nursery, children's church, and any additional benefits for attending the church.)

- end -

SAMPLE 51/2 x 81/2 HANDOUT

Marvin Yoder

Marvin Yoder grew up in the Old Order Amish Church, driving a horse and buggy and having no radio or television in his home. It is an exciting story how God made Himself known to a ten-year-old Amish boy and caused him to start traveling the path He ordained for his life. Marvin is a graduate of Rhema Bible Training Center in Broken Arrow, Oklahoma. Since graduating from Rhema in 1984, Marvin has pastored several churches in Kansas and Illinois.

Presently Marvin conducts Word of Life Seminars, which are designed to build up and refresh the Body of Christ.

Marvin's meetings will:

- Impart knowledge to help you be successful in life.
- Equip you to accomplish your God-given assignment.
- Refresh and refire you for effective ministry.

WHAT:

WHERE:

WHEN:

SAMPLE CONTACT RECORD SHEET

CHURCH _____

ADDRESS _____

CITY _____ ST _____ ZIP _____

PASTOR _____ WIFE _____

CHURCH PHONE _____ HOME PHONE _____

SECRETARY _____ CONGREGATION SIZE _____

INITIAL CONTACT DATE _____

SEND: ☐ Brochure   ☐ Tape   ☐ References   ☐ Other_____

RESPONSE: ☐ Yes ☐ No   ☐ Not now   ☐ Other_____

RECORD OF COMMUNICATION

DATE   MEETING

DATE(S)

_____ ☐ TELEPHONE ☐ MAIL ☐ VISIT

_____ ☐ TELEPHONE ☐ MAIL ☐ VISIT

_____ ☐ TELEPHONE ☐ MAIL ☐ VISIT

_____ ☐ TELEPHONE ☐ MAIL ☐ VISIT

_____ ☐ TELEPHONE ☐ MAIL ☐ VISIT

_____ ☐ TELEPHONE ☐ MAIL ☐ VISIT

_____ ☐ TELEPHONE ☐ MAIL ☐ VISIT

_____ ☐ TELEPHONE ☐ MAIL ☐ VISIT

_____ ☐ TELEPHONE ☐ MAIL ☐ VISIT

_____ ☐ TELEPHONE ☐ MAIL ☐ VISIT

_____ ☐ TELEPHONE ☐ MAIL ☐ VISIT

_____ ☐ TELEPHONE ☐ MAIL ☐ VISIT

_____ ☐ TELEPHONE ☐ MAIL ☐ VISIT

_____ ☐ TELEPHONE ☐ MAIL ☐ VISIT

_____ ☐ TELEPHONE ☐ MAIL ☐ VISIT

_____ ☐ TELEPHONE ☐ MAIL ☐ VISIT

_____ ☐ TELEPHONE ☐ MAIL ☐ VISIT

_____ ☐ TELEPHONE ☐ MAIL ☐ VISIT

_____ ☐ TELEPHONE ☐ MAIL ☐ VISIT

SAMPLE LETTER OF THANKS

(Date)

Pastor   (Name)
(Church Name)
(Address)
(City, State & Zip)

Dear Pastor _____ (Name) _____ ,

I wanted to write and tell you how much we appreciated the opportunity to minister in your church on _____ (Date) _____ . Your people were eager to receive the Word of God, and it was a pleasure to minister to them by the anointing of the Holy Spirit. I hope the ministry that took place will help accomplish the vision God has given you to do.

Thank you also for the offering you gave us, the motel room, and the meals you provided for us. A special thanks for the basket of fruit that you gave us. We were greatly blessed by it. The fellowship with you and your people was very special and edifying to me. May God's richest and best blessings be yours as you minister in His anointing.

I have enclosed an RMAI form for you to complete and mail in the stamped, pre-addressed envelope. Thank you for doing this for me.

Times of refreshing,

Marvin Yoder

Marvin Yoder

Printed Literature & Audio Products

Books and Tapes:
To Be or Not To Be?

Newsletters: Good News or
Bad News?

Mailing Lists & Information

14

Books and Tapes: To Be or Not To Be?

Having your own books and tapes can cause you to enter into a new realm of the traveling ministry. This lesson contains general guidelines, practical advice, and helpful hints to aid you if you decide to produce audiotape albums or publish your books.

DEVELOPING YOUR AUDIOTAPE MINISTRY

The following is a list of things you will need (equipment, supplies, etc.) if you decide to have an audiotape ministry.

1. Use only high quality master tapes to record your message.
2. You will need a supply of blank audiotapes which are available from various sources.
3. Labels with your ministry name and logo on them are necessary to put on your audiotapes.
4. You also need audiotape albums to package your audiotape series in order to sell them. Usually these albums are available from the same source that sells audiotapes.
5. Along with the audiotape albums, you must have a cover designed and printed that can be inserted into the front of the audiotape album.
6. You will also need a quality dual audiotape deck for recording and editing purposes.
7. You need a quality audiotape duplicator to produce your tapes.
8. Finally, you will need a bulk audiotape eraser.

Some of the advantages to having an audiotape ministry include:

1. It is another avenue to reach people with the Gospel.
2. It gives you the ability to reach a part of the world you may never visit personally.

3. It gives your ministry a new dimension or image and helps people raise their level of expectation toward your ministry.

Some of the disadvantages in having an audiotape ministry include:

1. It is a lot of work to edit and present a good quality tape.
2. It means carrying boxes of books and tapes with you when traveling.
3. It creates a need for greater cash flow in your ministry.
4. It is time-consuming to duplicate tapes, label them, and package them.

There are companies who specialize in putting together a tape package for ministries who don't have the necessary equipment to manufacture their own tapes. This service includes tape editing, duplication, and album cover and label design. You need to supply them with a good quality master tape and tell them what you want. I've listed one company that specializes in this service.

Cassette Outlet

714 W. Kenosha

Broken Arrow, OK 74012

918-251-0477 or 1-800-752-5346

There are various companies that can supply you with all kinds of items for your audiotape ministry such as

Personal Notes

blank tapes, albums, master tapes, labels, duplicating machines, and recording equipment. Here are two established companies from whom you can purchase the items that you may need to operate your audiotape ministry.

Church Cassette Co-op

600 Kenrick

Houston, TX 77060

1-800-683-3888 or 281-447-3888

Cassette Outlet

714 W. Kenosha

Broken Arrow, OK 74012

918-251-0477 or 1-800-752-5346

You should use only high quality master tapes to record your messages because your audiotapes are a representation of your ministry. Often you will have to instruct the sound person in the church where you're speaking how to adjust the sound equipment so that it is best suited for your voice.

Usually audiotape albums that contain two to six tapes will sell better than single or individual audiotapes. Also, by selling an album, you sell more tapes, which gives you a greater margin of profit and income.

Audiotapes often sell in direct proportion to the quality of your album cover. A quality album cover design creates eye appeal and helps people consider the message on the tapes. You may need to get some professional advice or help in the area of graphic design if you have no expertise in designing album covers. Hiring a professional is usually worth the fee you pay for his or her services. Remember, "price" is a one-time fee, while "cost" can last a life time.

DEVELOPING YOUR BOOK MINISTRY

There are a number of options you can pursue when considering a book ministry. Are you going to publish your book yourself, or are you going to present your manuscript to a publishing company and let them do it for you? Both self-publishing and finding a publishing company to publish your book have their benefits.

If you self-publish your book, you have to pay all of your costs up front, and you are responsible for distributing your book. However, you will probably be able to get your book into print and on the market faster and have a greater margin of profit per book copy that is sold than if you were to let a publishing company handle your book.

If you can find a publishing company to publish your book, you do not have to worry about up-front costs or distributing your book. Generally, they will have their own distribution network and take care of all sales. As the author, you would receive a royalty from the publishing company for every book that is sold. The amount you would receive per copy would be much lower than if you self-published your book. Usually, the publishing company

Personal Notes

Personal Notes

will sell a lot more copies through their distribution network than you can sell by yourself, so the total amount you receive from your books may be more than if you self-published your book.

Here are two companies who can help you self-publish your books. These are companies that do everything for you — from transcribing your message from an audiotape and typesetting your book to designing the book cover. Payment plans vary from company to company.

Press Group

7450 E. 46th Pl.

Tulsa, OK 74145

918-663-6655

Morris Publishing

3212 E. Hwy. 30

P.O. Box 2110

Kearney, NE 68848

1-800-650-7888

You will have to decide what kind of books that you want to print. There are several styles of bindings, covers, and sizes to choose from. Usually the purpose for your book will dictate the type of book style you will use. Here are some examples of book styles and the kind of information that usually is found in each one.

1. **Study guides** — mostly how-to manuals, Bible study material, or Bible school syllabuses — usually in an 8" x 11" size.
2. **Mini-books** (3" x 5") are an inexpensive way to print your message. There is not much profit margin in mini-books unless you print huge quantities of them.
3. **Paperback books** come in various sizes, from 5" x 8" to 3" x 5" slimline. Paperbacks are by far the style that most authors and publishers use for their books.

If you are doing a very low volume of books, or you are putting together seminar material, you may want to consider desk-top publishing as way to put your books together. This method involves doing everything on your computer and in your office. This will involve a lot of time and equipment. A partial list of equipment that you may need to do desk-top publishing would include the following:

1. A computer with good desk-top publishing software and an inkjet or laser printer to print your book.
2. A saddle stapler or a GBC Binding Machine to bind the books.
3. A heavy duty paper cutter to trim the edges of your book.

Personal Notes

Personal Notes

CONCLUSION

Having a book and tape ministry may seem like a lot of work, but it also has great rewards for you. You can have satisfaction knowing that you can affect future generations with the Gospel of Jesus Christ through your books and tapes.

15

Newsletters: Good News or Bad News?

Having a newsletter will give you the opportunity to minister to people that you do not personally meet. The printed page is one of the best avenues to share and communicate the Good News of Jesus Christ.

This lesson takes a look at the pros and cons of producing a newsletter, evaluates the necessity of having a newsletter, and reveals some tips on putting a newsletter together.

IDENTIFY YOUR PURPOSE

Here are some questions you should try to answer before you start sending out a newsletter. This will enable you to determine the content of your newsletter and know exactly what you want to accomplish with your newsletter.

- Is it to communicate your vision?
- Is it for reporting the events and progress of your ministry?
- Is it for fund-raising purposes?
- Is it for a one-time purpose, or is it going to be periodical? If periodical, how often is the newsletter to be mailed out?
- Can your ministry afford to print and mail a newsletter? Do you have a large enough group of supporters and interested people to justify doing this?

Here are some of the reasons and advantages you should consider if you are thinking about mailing out a newsletter:

1. It can be a vehicle to communicate your vision. Since communication is the key to relationships, your newsletter can play a vital role in telling people what you are attempting to do.
2. It can keep your people and supporters updated concerning your ministry. People will stay interested in your ministry if you keep them updated on the progress of the various projects that you are accomplishing.

3. It can serve as an avenue to raise funds to meet the needs of the ministry. Most people will give to a project or ministry if they know what is going on and that there is a need they can help with.

4. It can be used to share a message even though you cannot be there in person. Your newsletter should be designed as a valuable tool for touching people's lives with the Gospel. Never underestimate the power of the printed page in reaching someone for Christ.

Here are some of the disadvantages you should know about if you are going to produce a newsletter.

1. Mailing your newsletter out on a regular basis requires you to meet deadlines. You cannot send out a newsletter on a sporadic basis and have very good response from the people who receive it.

2. If you are producing the newsletter yourself, you may have to have some creative skills in order to produce a quality newsletter.

3. An outlay of cash is needed to print and mail the newsletter. Therefore, printing and mailing newsletters will require a greater cash flow in your ministry.

4. Additional staff or professional help may need to be hired. If you cannot design and put together a professional newsletter, you are better off hiring someone with professional skills to do it for you.

Personal Notes

Remember that your newsletter is representative of you and your ministry.

TIPS, HINTS, AND ADVICE IN PRODUCING A NEWSLETTER

If producing a newsletter is not an area in which you have adequate knowledge and skill, by all means get help from someone who knows what he's doing. Our ignorance is never so obvious as when we put it into print. Know your limits, and beyond that hire a professional.

The following information is some general guidelines for people to consider when they are attempting to lay out their own newsletter.

1. Consult with a print shop in your area. They can give you advice on how to lay out a newsletter, give you an idea of cost, as well as give you typesetting information.

2. It may be beneficial to for you talk to a graphic artist who has expertise in designing logos and in creating newsletters.

Tips in design:

1. Use a simple, bold design that allows the text to be read at a glance. In this fast-paced world people do not spend a lot of time reading things that are sent to them. Therefore your newsletter must be designed so that readers are able to very quickly comprehend what you are saying.

2. Use a Sans Serif type, such as Universal, for headlines and the subheadings of your newsletter. Use a Serif type, such as Times New Roman, in the body of your newsletter to enhance readability.

3. Try to limit the different kinds of fonts you use in your newsletter to no more than two or three. This will help make your newsletter more readable and less cluttered.

4. Use lots of white space. Have plenty of room around your headlines and around your articles. Do not clutter your page; it lessens readability.

5. Use two or three columns wherever you can instead of running your articles completely across the page. This makes your newsletter much easier to read.

6. Another way to attract attention to your newsletter is to use two colors of ink. Make your headlines and main titles, lines, and boxes one color; make your text another color.

7. Use colored paper instead of white to help catch the reader's attention. You can literally help improve people's reception of your newsletter by the colors you use. If you are making an announcement, you might choose a bold, bright fluorescent color to grab a person's attention and interest. Use various pastel col-

Personal Notes

Personal Notes

ors to create a more peaceful and inviting look. Determine the purpose of your newsletter, and then choose a color that reflects your purpose.

8. Printing your newsletter on specialty paper is another inexpensive way to have a two or three color newsletter. Various companies have already created and printed various multi-colored designs for newsletter layout. You simply fill in the blank spaces with your headlines and text with black ink from your computer. (See page 121 for a list of companies that offer specialty papers.)

SUGGESTIONS FOR DEALING WITH A PRINT SHOP

Do a "printer's run" on various colors if you're using another color besides black. A "printer's run" is when you choose the colors you want, and the print shop prints your newsletter when they are using your specific colors on another job. This helps keep your cost down, because it eliminates a washing charge to change ink colors in the presses.

For a cost-effective two-color newsletter, especially if your newsletter is being printed periodically, have it designed so that some basic elements such as headlines, boxes, and lines will remain the same. Print a year's worth of copies of this portion of your newsletter using color ink.

Use a "printer's run" to do this if possible. Then have your text and information for each issue printed in black. This will not cost you as much as having two colors printed each issue.

See the sample of a newsletter on the page 120 for more tips in design and layout.

CONCLUSION

A newsletter can raise people's awareness of your ministry and at the same time be a great blessing to them as they read what you have to say.

Personal Notes

SAMPLE NEWSLETTER LAYOUT

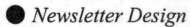

● *Newsletter Design*

Creative Designs And Strategies For Your Newsletter *

TIPS

READ ME FIRST!

Did you? If you started reading here, you're probably responding to visual tactics purposely designed to attract you to what would be the lead article in a real newspaper. Bold contrasts of scale, weight, and color make the head above and the drop cap left stand out from the rest of the page. The larger, wider introductory type is inviting because it looks easier to read. Placement, too, brought you here — readers of English are conditioned to start reading somewhere near the upper left-hand corner of the page, underneath the masthead.

You probably looked there first to find a clue; the "Read Me First!" headline did the rest. By using simple design tactics you can cause your reader to respond in predetermined ways. Or in other words, you can guide the eyes of your reader to specific locations in your design. You can make your newsletter communicate quicker and more directly by using this sort of low-cost typographic and design strategy instead of expensive color and printing techniques.

Type: the first tactic

This page is made up of little more than *type*. Different sizes, weights, and shapes of type give the page it's texture and interest.

All the variations are accomplished through the use of only two type families. Times Roman, the lightweight serif text you are reading now, was chosen for its comfortable, familiar look, and Impact Bold was used for the headlines.

Boxing Me In

☞ When you want to call attention to something on the page, enclosing it in a box can really make it stand out. Use this technique to underline a major point, introduce a new idea, or add supplementary information. The hand in this box is another trick to convince you that this is important and to read it right away.

* This newsletter design and tips are adapted from a handout given by Brian Torvik during Continuing Education Seminar at Rhema Bible Training Center in Broken Arrow, Oklahoma.

SOURCES FOR SPECIALTY PAPER AND PRINTING

Personal Notes

Paper Sources:

QUILL COMPANY	1-800-789-1331	
100 Schelter Rd.	1-800-789-8955 (Fax)	
Lincolnshire, IL 60069-3621		

PAPER DIRECT   1-800-272-7377
100 Plaza Drive   201-271-9601 (Fax)
Secaucus, NJ 07094-3606

PREMIER PAPERS   1-800-843-0414
P.O. Box 64785   1-800-526-3029 (Fax)
St. Paul, MN 55164

BEAVER PRINTS   1-814-742-6070
305 Main St.   1-800-232-8374 (Fax)
Bellwood, PA 16617

VIKING OFFICE PRODUCTS 1-800-421-1222
4782 Mulhauser Rd.   1-800-762-7329 (Fax)
P.O. Box 465644
Cincinnati, OH 45246-5644

**Full Color Printing
Sources:**

RAPIDOCOLOR   1-800-872-7436
705 E. Union St.   610-344-0506 (Fax)
West Chester, PA 19382

FLASH PRINT   1-800-374-6114
35 Bath St.   518-885-2576 (Fax)
Ballston Spa, NY 12020

16

Mailing Lists & Information

The mail that some people receive can be a matter of life or death to them. For this reason, what you decide to send through the mail is a ministry decision as well as a business decision. Here are some facts about the mail service that can help you be more effective in using the mail as an avenue of ministry.

- Your ministry mail can go where you can not personally go.
- The letters, newsletters, tapes, and books that you send in the mail can represent you and Christ in various places at the same time.

- Your ministry mail can minister the Good News of Christ to people.
- Using the mail system is a valid form of ministry to people.

Sending the Good News through the mail in the best way possible necessitates having a working knowledge of the postal system and its requirements. Developing and knowing how to take care of your mailing list is also very important.

THE U.S. POSTAL SERVICE

The U.S. Postal Service has various manuals, pamphlets, and bulletins available that contain vital information for nonprofit organizations. This information can help you be as cost-effective as possible and help you avoid doing something illegal. Several of the items that are available from the U.S. Postal Service are listed below.

The Domestic Mail Manual (Annual fee with updates)
Obtain from: Superintendent of Documents
U.S. Printing Office
Washington D.C. 20402
202-783-3238

Postal Bulletins (Bi-weekly)
Obtain from: Superintendent of Documents
U.S. Printing Office
Washington D.C. 20402
202-783-3238

Memo to Mailers (Monthly)
Obtain at:
P.O. Box 1
Lynwood, NJ 08221

Publication 201 (Consumer's Guide to Postal

Services & Products)

Obtain at:
Your local Post Office

Publication 417 (Nonprofit Standard Mail Eligibility)
Obtain at:
Your local Post Office

Publication 49 (Standard Mail (A) Preparation)
Obtain at:
Your local Post Office

Publication 25 (Designing Letter and Reply Mail)
Obtain at:
Your local Post Office

Ask your local Postmaster for additional mail publications that you may need.

DIFFERENT CLASSES OF MAIL AND THEIR REGULATIONS

The U.S. Postal Service has various classifications of mail. Each classification is designed to meet certain purposes and needs of those who are sending mail. There are specific regulations that apply to each classification. The following is a list of the various classifications and some of the regulations. For more details, you may obtain Publication 201 from the U.S. Postal Service.

Personal Notes

Personal Notes

First-Class Mail

- For personal letters, postcards, greeting cards, and for sending money orders or checks, use first-class mail.
- For prompt delivery, use first-class mail. Usually, this is the fastest mode of postal service except for special services like Express Mail or Priority Mail.

Periodical Mail

- Only newspapers and magazines can be mailed at periodical mail rates.
- Only publishers and registered news agents may use periodical mail rates.

Standard Mail

- There are two types of standard mail rates:
    1. Regular standard mail (for retailers, catalogers, and advertisers to promote their products and services).
    2. Nonprofit standard mail (for nonprofit organizations meeting certain qualifications).
- An annual permit must be purchased for standard mail. Currently the permit costs $100.
- An imprint permit may also need to be purchased for a one-time fee, currently $100.
- The minimum volume necessary to use standard mail rates is 200 pieces or 50 pounds per mailing,

and the pieces must weigh less than 16 ounces each.

- All pieces mailed at the standard mail rate must be identical in content and weight. No personalization is allowed, nor are you allowed to mail another organization's mail under your permit.
- Mailing frequency to maintain a standard mail permit is as follows:
  - Once a year for regular standard mail rates.
  - Twice a year for nonprofit standard mail rates.
- Presorting is required for all standard mail. The more you sort, the more you save. You can presort your mail according to state, 3/5 digit zip code, or carrier route.
- Your mail must be properly labeled when mailing at the standard mail rates to show what each package is sorted by, whether it be state, 3/5 digit zip code, or carrier route. These labels are available at your local post office.
- Current standard mail rates are as follows:

  Regular bulk rates (letter size)
(1)	Basic presort	23.5¢/piece
(2)	3/5 digit zip code presort	20.7¢/piece

  Nonprofit bulk rates (letter size)
(1)	Basic presort	16.9¢/piece
(2)	3/5 digit zip code presort	14.2¢/piece

Personal Notes

Standard Mail (B)

- This is for packages weighing 1-70 pounds mailed in the continental United States.
- Library rate (for books and audio or videotapes) is also fourth class.
- Standard mail (B) rates are less expensive than first-class rates.

MAILING LISTS FOR YOUR MINISTRY MAIL

As you continue in the ministry, you will probably develop many relationships with people with whom you will want to stay in touch. One of the ways you will probably stay in touch with them is by mail. As you compile the names and addresses of these contacts, you will soon have your own ministry database and mailing list.

Concentrate on building your ministry mailing list with the people you have developed a relationship with or with the people who have expressed an interest in your ministry. Avoid getting people's names and addresses by questionable practices. Some unethical or illegal ways to add to your mailing list include getting names and addresses in the following ways:

- From people who have not given you prior approval to put them on your mailing list.

- Using the church directory where you conducted your meetings.
- From checks people give you when they buy your books and audio products.
- Using mailing lists or membership directories of other ministries without their permission.

Be careful to maintain and guard your mailing list. Your mailing list is a valuable asset of your ministry. Various organizations will offer to buy mailing lists from other organizations; however, it is not a good idea to let other organizations have access to them. It may be wise to not let employees have access to your mailing lists without guidelines concerning the use of them. For a small cost, you can obtain a helpful little book entitled <u>How To Compile and Maintain a Mailing List</u>.

Obtain from: **Quill Corporation**
100 S. Schelter Rd.
Lincolnshire, IL 60069
312-634-4850

You can stay current with your mailing list by putting "address correction" on all of your ministry mail. This also helps to cut down on the cost of mailing to addresses that are no longer valid and helps you eliminate duplicate addresses in your mailing list.

Personal Notes

Personal Notes

CONCLUSION

How you deal with your mail is important. It is a representation of your ministry. Remember that using the mail can be an avenue of ministry. When you send your ministry material in the mail, it contains the Gospel of Jesus Christ and will minister life and healing to those who receive it.

Traveling Tips for the Ministry

Methods of Travel

The Hotel Game

17

Methods Of Travel

In the beginning stages, when a traveling minister is just starting to travel, he will usually drive his existing vehicle to the meetings he has scheduled. Whatever vehicle you use to travel to your meetings, always do the best you can. People may judge your ministry and determine whether or not they will receive from your ministry by your outward appearance and the vehicle you drive.

Use your faith and trust God to help you obtain the best vehicle your budget will allow. I am not saying you should drive an expensive luxury car. It doesn't even have to be a new vehicle, but your vehicle should be the best

Personal Notes

it possibly can be. It should look good, be dependable, and be clean and neat. Nothing creates a negative image of a traveling minister the way a dirty and untidy vehicle does.

Maintain and take care of your vehicle. Pastors have to trust God for buildings in which to hold church services, and traveling ministers have to trust God for the vehicle they need in order to get to their meetings.

DRIVING TO YOUR MEETINGS

A new road atlas is a good investment for you to make every year, especially if you drive to most of your meetings. Roads are constantly being upgraded and repaired. A new road map may show you improved roads, new interstate or toll roads, completed by-pass routes around cities, or two-lane roads that have been changed to multi-lane highways.

There are several computer software programs that have maps of the whole United States on them, plus close-ups of cities and their streets to help you plan the best route to your destination. Some of these programs also give travel advice, such as listing restaurants and hotels along your route. Most of these programs cost less than a hundred dollars. Check your local computer or office supply store to see what they have available.

Your vehicle is a tool to help you fulfill God's call. Again, regular maintenance is a must to help avoid costly emergency repairs on the road. Regular maintenance will not cost as much in the long run as emergency repairs on the road will cost.

Tips to better traveling:

- Give your vehicle a last-minute inspection before taking a trip.
- Properly inflate your tires to get maximum performance from them.
- Keep some wrenches and other basic tools in your vehicle in case minor repairs are needed.
- Carry a roll of duct tape with you to help temporarily repair leaks and hoses.
- Keep several rubber tie-down straps in the vehicle. They can be used for a variety of things.
- A set of jumper cables may be a good thing to carry along.
- Check the fluid levels and the condition of your belts in your vehicle before taking a trip.

If your family is traveling with you, remember that close quarters in a vehicle can cause tension in relationships. Take some activities (games, books, etc.) along for the children. Perhaps you can get a television with a built-in VCR so the kids can watch videos as you travel. Another idea is to stop at a city park as you drive through a town and take a short break to let the family run off some energy.

Personal Notes

FLYING TO YOUR MEETINGS

There are advantages and disadvantages to flying to your meetings. Explore the pros and cons of driving versus flying and make your decisions accordingly.

When calculating whether you will save time by flying versus driving to your meetings, be sure to consider check-in time, waiting time, boarding time, time to claim your baggage, as well as time to rent a car if needed. Usually, if you can drive to your destination in less than five hours, you will not save any significant amount of time by flying to your meetings.

Most of the time airline tickets and related costs are up front, out of pocket expenses for you. As a general rule, a church will not reimburse you for traveling expenses until after you have finished the meetings. This will require your ministry to have a greater cash flow, and it may also require additional planning on your part.

There are several classifications that most airlines offer to the people who fly with them. The two classifications that most people are familiar with are first-class and coach fare. Some airlines also offer a business class, which is similar to first class, especially on flights that go overseas. Business class may not cost as much as first class, but usually costs more than coach fare.

Generally, a traveling minister should fly coach fare, unless the church where you are ministering has voluntarily bought a first-class ticket for you. Otherwise you should only fly first class when you are paying for it, and do not require the church to reimburse you for it. Do your best to keep your airline costs as low as possible.

Make use of SuperSaver or Frequent Flyer programs that airlines offer so you can qualify for discounts. This usually takes some advanced planning. There are various programs that the different airlines offer, as well as specials that they offer at various times. Educate yourself on the different programs that airlines offer, since airline rates are constantly changing.

There are web sites on the Internet where a person can go to purchase airline tickets, often at a discount. Some web sites allow you to offer a bid on a flight you want to take, and you can sometimes save a significant amount of money by doing this. However, if you make a bid on an airline fare, be prepared to be flexible in your schedule. Other airline information is also available on the Internet. Be sure to check all confirmation information when it is sent to you to be sure you have received what you ordered. You should also be aware that participating in the programs offered on the Internet will usually require the use of your credit card.

Some airlines offer credit cards that give you free mileage for every dollar that you charge on them. This can help you save on airline costs and other related items.

Personal Notes

Consider booking the next-to-last flight out of town to your destination. This gives you a backup plan in case of an emergency, traffic jams, bad weather, etc. and allows you to take the last flight out of town in case you miss your original flight.

Should you fly commercial or get your own private airplane? George Otis, former President of Lear Jet Corporation, gives us this advice, "Commercial airplanes are required to pass regular safety inspections, while private planes are not as frequently inspected. Therefore, unless your time schedule demands a private airplane, and you have the money and personnel to give regular safety inspections, you should fly commercial." (As a side note, when George Otis had his own ministry, he still flew commercial.)

Here are some things to consider when flying to your meetings:

1. Your time is valuable. How much time will it take to drive the distance in your vehicle versus flying, and what could you be doing with that time?

2. In addition to airline costs, there are either taxi or rental car costs, unless the church where your ministering will provide you with transportation.

3. Call at least three travel agencies to price shop for the cheapest airfare to and from your destination.

4. Flying on certain days of the week is often less expensive than flying on others. Check with your travel agency or airline to see which days are best.

5. In major cities with several airports, check the price of flying into each airport. Flying into some airports is less expensive than flying into others even though they are in the same city.

CONCLUSION

Knowing how to travel smart will enable you to arrive at your destination on time and also keep your costs at a minimum. This will help you be a good witness and bring glory to God in your traveling ministry.

Personal Notes

18

The Hotel Game

As a traveling minister, you will soon find an occasion where you have to stay in a hotel. Finding a room for the night, dealing with hotels, and sleeping in hotels is a fact of life for a traveling minister. It becomes essential for a traveling minister to know how to deal with hotels, how hotels operate, and how to get the best deal possible when making a reservation.

This lesson contains information concerning getting the best deal possible when making a reservation, what to do while you are staying at a hotel, and how to take care of your hotel bill correctly.

_____

_____

_____

_____

_____

_____

_____

_____

_____

_____

_____

_____

_____

_____

_____

_____

_____

_____

GETTING A HOTEL ROOM

An important thing to keep in mind when making a reservation is that at a hotel you have to ask for everything you want. Usually hotels will not tell you of their own volition about any specials or discounts they may be offering. Do not hesitate to ask about discounts or specials or for any extra items that you want in your room.

Some hotels have cheaper rates on certain days of the week than other days. Some hotels may also give a discount if you stay at the hotel for a certain number of days. Again, ask the hotel where you are staying about this.

Instead of calling the corporate headquarters for a reservation, try directly calling the local hotel where you will be staying. They can tell you about any local specials or discounts as well as the discounts that are offered throughout the whole hotel chain.

Periodically, some major hotel chains have a program or a special discount where they give people a free night after they have stayed in their hotels for a certain number of nights. Check with the hotel where you're staying to see if they have a program like this, especially if you are staying at the same hotel a number of times.

Contact the hotel sales office and ask for their corporate rates, economy rooms, super saver rooms, etc. Do this especially if you are coming through several times a year. Many hotels will give their corporate rate and discounts to ministries the same as they do to other business travelers.

Often during their busy season, hotels will over-book their rooms by at least ten percent because they know their approximate cancellation rate. This helps them to have all the rooms rented out for the night. However, as a traveler, you need to know what implications this has for you.

When you make a reservation at a hotel, always make sure that you get a confirmation number for your room from the hotel clerk. If the hotel does not give you a confirmation number, be sure to get the person's name with whom you made the reservation. If a hotel has over-booked their rooms, they may attempt to give your room to someone else, especially if you did not have a confirmation number or have your room confirmed with a credit card.

If you are arriving at the hotel after 6:00 P.M. (4:00 P.M. if you are staying at a resort hotel), you should always confirm your room with a credit card. If you don't have a credit card, make arrangements with the hotel ahead of time so you can mail in a pre-payment on your room to confirm it. If you do not guarantee your room with a credit card or pre-payment, and you arrive late, the hotel may assume you aren't coming and give your room to someone else, especially if they are over-booked.

Personal Notes

Personal Notes

When you check into the hotel you should always verify your room rate to make sure it is the same rate that was quoted to you when you made the reservations. Sometimes a hotel will try to tell you that their rates have changed or that their personnel made a mistake and that they cannot give you the rate that was quoted to you. However, you have every right to quietly but firmly insist on the original room rate. If the desk clerk will not honor the original rate, ask to speak with the manager about your room rate.

There are various organizations that offer discount hotel rates to their members. Two of them are listed below. Usually there is an annual fee to join the organization. These organizations offer discounts on various things, such as hotel rates, rental car fees, long distance telephone service, air fares, etc. Usually you have to make your reservation farther in advance if you use the services offered by these organizations. Be aware that some hotels may only honor the discount rates through these organizations on certain days of the week or at certain times of the year.

CLERGY CARD

P.O. Box 8338

South Bend, IN 46660

1-800-8CLERGY

CLERGY TRAVEL, INC.

1443 Del Prado Blvd. Suite A & B

Cape Coral, FL 33990

1-800-458-8281 or 813-574-7755

YOUR HOTEL ROOM

As a traveling minister, you will probably spend a lot of lonely hours in your hotel room. Being alone brings its own temptations. The challenge is to stay disciplined and make those hours productive for the Kingdom of God.

It is important to pray over your room when you get there. Take authority in Jesus' Name over any evil spirits that may have had permission to be there due to the activities of the previous tenants. Ask God to cover you with the blood of Jesus Christ for protection.

Be careful with the television in your room. Some ministers can trace their sexual problems back to when they were alone with television and movies in hotel rooms. There are several things you can do with your television to help avoid temptations:

1. Ask at the hotel desk to send someone to take the television out of your room.
2. Ask at the hotel desk if it is possible to block out the channels with bad programming on the television in your room.

Here are some safety tips while staying at a hotel (courtesy of the American Hotel and Motel Association):

1. When arriving or returning to your hotel room late at night, use the main entrance to the hotel. Be observant and look around before walking through parking lots.

Personal Notes

2. Don't answer the door of your hotel room without verifying who it is. If the person states that they are an employee, call the front desk and ask if an employee is supposed to have access to your room and for what purpose.

3. Close your hotel room door securely whenever you are in the room. Use all the locking devices provided.

4. Don't display your hotel room keys needlessly in public or leave them in a restaurant, at the hotel swimming pool, or other places where they can easily be stolen.

5. Do not draw attention to yourself by displaying large amounts of money or expensive jewelry.

6. It may be a good idea to keep all of your valuables in the hotel safe deposit box.

7. Check to see that any sliding glass doors or windows in your room and any connecting room doors are locked and have sufficient security devices to ensure your safety while you are there.

8. When unlocking your hotel room door, be aware of who is near you. If a person with questionable intentions is close by, go back to the front desk and ask for someone to go with you to your room.

YOUR HOTEL BILL

You should always ask for a copy of the hotel bill when you are checking out of your hotel room, even though the church may be paying for it. Make sure that the charges on the bill are correct. Make sure that the hotel did not make a mistake or put someone else's charges on your bill. Serious questions may be raised in the mind of the pastor of the church where you have been ministering if incorrect or questionable charges are on your hotel bill.

If incorrect charges have been put on your hotel bill, insist that the charges be taken completely off the bill. Do not let them leave the charge on your bill and show a cancellation or a credit for it. Insist that they take the charge completely off of your bill so that the pastor will see an accurate account of the charges that you incurred when you stayed there. You may want to ask for an extra copy of the bill to give to the pastor personally so that he can compare it with the bill that he will receive from the hotel.

Never leave your telephone calls on the hotel bill for the church to pay. Even if a pastor tells you to do so, it is usually not a good idea. Most of the time the pastor does not realize how many long distance telephone calls a traveling minister may need to make.

Personal Notes

One way to save money on your telephone bill is by using phone cards. There are a number of phone cards available with very good long distance rates. This helps you avoid the extremely high rates the hotel charges you when you dial out directly from your room.

You should not leave your laundry charges on your bill for the church to pay, unless previous arrangements were made by the church specifically for them. These charges were for your personal things, and the church should not be required to pay them.

Do not charge food on your hotel bill and leave it for the church to pay, unless the church has made previous arrangements for you to do so. When you do charge food to the hotel bill that the church is paying, be sure to eat conservatively. You should refrain from getting the most expensive item on the menu. Treat the church like you would want to be treated.

CONCLUSION

Hotel bills can be a big-ticket item for a traveling ministry. Price shopping and being aware of how hotels operate can help you decrease your hotel costs and help safeguard you against those who may try to take advantage of you.

Proper Ethics in the Traveling Ministry

19

Getting Along With the Local Church

There are many traveling ministries functioning in the Body of Christ. They each have their way of conducting their ministry. Not all of them operate the same because they do not have the same calling or purpose. However, there are some general rules of ethics and integrity that all traveling ministers should use to govern their lives, their conduct, and their ministry.

The Scriptures teach by principle and example certain ethics and protocol that a wise and successful traveling minister will recognize and adhere to. Doing so will enhance your ministry, increase the favor and receptivity that others will extend toward you, and help ensure your longevity in the traveling ministry.

One of the first foundational rules of ethics is to recognize the different types of ministries that God has set into the Body of Christ.

> **EPHESIANS 4:11**
> **And he gave some, apostles; and some, prophets; and some, evangelists; and some, pastors and teachers.**

God has given both traveling ministers and pastors as leadership ministries to the Church.

SIMILARITIES BETWEEN TRAVELING MINISTERS AND PASTORS

- Both are leadership gifts given to the Body of Christ.
- Both are called by God to function in the Body of Christ.
- Both serve the common cause of touching people for Christ.
- Both types of ministry are necessary to the Church
    1. To bring to perfection the Body of Christ.
    2. To equip the saints for the work of the ministry.

EPHESIANS 4:12
For the PERFECTING of the saints, for the work of the ministry, for the EDIFYING of the Body of Christ.

DIFFERENCES BETWEEN TRAVELING MINISTERS AND PASTORS

Traveling ministers and pastors are distinct in their gifts and anointings. Each type of ministry looks at the same problem or situation from a different viewpoint. Neither is necessarily wrong. Both should be tolerant of each other's views and remember that they work for the same Master and belong to the same Body of Christ even though they have different functions and roles to fulfill.

The traveling minister and the pastor should not be compared with each other. They are not the same, and they do not have the same anointing for ministry. It is usually very unwise for ministers to compare their gifts and callings with those of other ministers.

Pastors cannot supply the total spiritual leadership needed by the Church. Christ gave five leadership gifts to the Church for the perfecting of the saints, not just one gift. Pastors should value traveling ministers, because traveling ministers are gifted with different anointings and abilities to produce results and minister in the Body of Christ in such a way that the pastor is not capable of doing.

Personal Notes

Traveling ministries do not have the ability nor the anointing to pastor a church. They do not have the grace of God to stay in one place for a long period of time and minister to the same group of people time and again. Traveling ministers should remember that the pastor has to stay with the local people after they are gone, and therefore they should not leave a mess for the pastor to clean up.

Traveling ministers should submit to pastoral authority while they are in the local church, even if the pastor tells them to do something different than what they "heard God" tell them to do. Even if traveling ministers have achieved some level of fame or are in the office of a prophet or apostle, they should still recognize the pastor as having been given the oversight of the local flock, and thus they should endeavor to work with the pastor.

Traveling ministers should remember that the local church is the "hand that feeds them." Sometimes the offerings that a traveling minister receives from a local church is all he has to live on. Therefore traveling ministers should avoid grumbling or bad-mouthing a church or a pastor.

A QUESTION OF HONOR

It is a matter of honor for a traveling minister and pastor to recognize each other's gifts and receive each other properly. The traveling minister and the pastor should work together for the sake of the anointing so that proper ministry can flow in the Body of Christ. (Remember, the redemption and maturity of people is why God has placed these ministry gifts into the Body of Christ.)

If a person will not receive or honor a certain ministry gift properly, it will hinder or limit what that person can receive from God. Such a person has limited himself in what God can give to him, not just through that particular vessel, but through other ministry gifts as well. Not only does it affect the spiritual progress of that person, it also affects how well the immediate family members progress spiritually.

EPHESIANS 4:1-3
I therefore, the prisoner of the Lord, beseech you that ye walk worthy of the vocation wherewith ye are called,
With all lowliness and meekness, with longsuffering, forbearing one another in love;
Endeavouring to keep the unity of the Spirit in the bond of peace.

The Apostle Paul encouraged all believers, including ministers, to walk or conduct themselves in a manner that is worthy of being a member in the Body of Christ. As people walk in this manner they will enjoy the benefits of being in the unity of the Spirit, and they will be able to

ROMANS 15:7
Wherefore receive ye one another, as Christ also received us to the glory of God.

Personal Notes

dwell in the peace of God. Some of the benefits they will enjoy include:

1. Receiving blessings and revelation from God.
2. Becoming properly equipped.
3. Receiving the anointing of God.
4. Ministering effectively with the correct motives.

CONCLUSION

Even though a person is in the traveling ministry, he is still a member of the universal Body of Christ. Traveling ministers should be hooked up with a local church and avoid being a "lone ranger." They should learn to value the local church and respect the different functions of the various members in it.

20

Ethics and the Traveling Minister

PART ONE

In this lesson we are going to discuss the proper ethics by which traveling ministers should conduct themselves. The word "ethics" comes from the Greek word "ethikos," which refers to the general character and ideals of a person and also involves principles of right conduct.

How a traveling minister deals with pastors and local churches is very important. Since traveling ministers will preach mostly in local churches, their attitude and conduct toward the local church needs to be correct, moral, and ethical.

KNOWING THE PASTOR

One of the keys to successful traveling ministry is to take a genuine interest in the pastor, his family, and his church. It can only help you as a traveling minister to take the time to find out basic information about the pastor's personality, what he like and dislikes, and his style of ministry. Make every effort to take an interest in the pastor as a person.

Often a pastor has no one in the local area that he can share his heart with and still be effective in his church. In some cases, a traveling minister can really help a pastor by showing that he is concerned and cares about the things the pastor has been going through. Sometimes pastors have family or ministry problems, and they need to talk with someone. There are times when the traveling minister is the only person they can talk to.

Consider a pastor's style of ministry as you determine how you will conduct your meetings. Make every effort to flow with the pastor as you minister the Word of God by the Holy Spirit to the people. The blessings of God flow freely as you minister together in unity and agreement. Some pastors are very laid back, and they will give you full liberty to do anything you want. Other pastors may want to know what you will preach and give you specific time limits, and they may even want to help you with the altar ministry.

ROMANS 15:7
Wherefore receive ye one another, as Christ also received us to the glory of God.

CONDUCTING YOUR MEETINGS ETHICALLY

As you conduct your meetings, keep in mind the goal of what you are doing. Your purpose should be to facilitate effective ministry to the people so they can receive what they need from God. You are a minister sent by God to minister to people. That should be your primary concern.

There may be times when you are tempted to do some things during the course of ministry in order to receive more money, such as talking about the things you desire to have, preaching on giving, prophesying to people to give money, or approaching people privately about giving an offering into your ministry. Take some time to make sure that your heart is right and that the reasons you do things are for ministry's sake, not for money's sake.

It is not a good idea to change dates with a church once you have a meeting scheduled with them, unless there is a clear understanding between you and the pastor. Sometimes you will have opportunities to go to other places to minister, and it would benefit you if you could change the dates on meetings that you have already scheduled. However, changing dates should not even be considered if the meeting dates are coming up in the near future. Be a person of your word and do what you promised.

Sometimes a pastor will grudgingly consent to changing dates so that you can go elsewhere. However,

Personal Notes

doing so may not create the best situation for him and his church. At best, it puts him in a position of having to explain to his people that you can't come when you were originally scheduled and will have to come at another time.

It is considerate to communicate your arrival and departure time in advance so the pastor can properly pre-pare for you. Contacting the pastor one to three weeks ahead of the meeting dates allows any last minute details to be worked out. It is a good idea to contact the pastor when you are approximately thirty minutes to an hour away so that he can be ready for you. You can also find out then where the pastor wants to meet you.

Be very considerate of the spiritual atmosphere in the service when deciding when to promote your books and tapes. The worship team may have worked very hard to bring the spiritual atmosphere to a high level of worship. At the height of worshipping God, the pastor may give you the service. That is not the time to do a book and tape com-mercial.

There are times when the atmosphere is set for ministry. Do not use the time when the anointing has manifested to promote your books and tapes. Some options to consider in determining when to do a tape and book commercial is to have someone do it during announcement times, or do it yourself after you are finished preaching the Word and ministering to the people.

As a traveling minister in a local church, do not receive your own offerings. It is wise for you and the pastor to have an understanding about the financial arrangements ahead of time. Once in a while a pastor may insist that he wants you to receive your own offering. But as a traveling minister you should never insist on taking your own offering in a church. Submit to what the pastor and you agree upon. Then believe God to meet your needs.

Limit the time that you preach. Someone once said, "Blessed are the short-winded for they shall be invited back." That may be more of a factor than most people realize. One older minister listened to a group of young ministers talking about how long they preach. Some said they preached an hour, others preached an hour and a half, and one minister even preached for two hours. Finally the senior minister said, "I've been listening to you say how long you preach, and I just have one question for you. Are you all really that good?"

How good of a preacher are you? Read a good book on the subject of effective preaching and communicating. Then evaluate your preaching abilities fairly. Make any adjustments that are necessary. Here are some other issues to consider when determining the length of your sermon.

1. Know when you have you said what God wants said. This is your most important goal, and it should be accomplished as quickly as possible.

Personal Notes

Personal Notes

2. What time limits has the pastor given you? Do your best to stay within his time frame.

3. How long can you keep the attention of the audience? Especially if you're having meetings every night during the week, it is a good idea to keep your sermons short. You will wear the people out if you preach a long time every evening.

4. Keep in mind that children may have to go to school the next day. People will probably attend your meetings during the week when school is in session more readily if they know you aren't going to preach a long time.

5. Consider the children's workers that have increased burdens in taking care of children in long meetings. In most local churches, having ample children's workers is difficult enough without having a long-winded traveling minister who doesn't consider the efforts and sacrifices made by the workers during special meetings.

6. If there are a lot of special things, such as announcements, baby dedications, communion, etc., being done in the church service prior to your preaching, you may want to omit part of your message so that your quitting time is within reason.

Do not preach on controversial subjects unless you have talked with the pastor first. Preaching on controversial issues seldom creates an atmosphere of good will. Your content may be right; however, it is just as important that the attitudes created by what you preach reflect the love of God. Most of the time it is better for the pastor to deal with difficult subjects because he knows the heartbeat his congregation.

1. When preaching on money, talk it over with the pastor first. Make sure the pastor and you have the same viewpoints about what you intend to say. You might give him a general outline of your sermon.

2. Stay away from the latest controversy in the Body of Christ unless you have encouragement and a solution for that local church. The best way to deal with these issues may be to share what you have received from the Lord with the pastor, and then let him bring it to the local church.

3. Be very careful about the subject of sex, especially oral sex, in a mixed audience where children are present. Often adults understand what is being said, but it can be very embarrassing for parents when their children ask them what the preacher meant by some comment he made on sexual issues. It may be better for the pastor to address

Personal Notes

Personal Notes

this subject, because he has a sensitive heart toward his people and knows them better than you do.

4. If you decide to talk about the rapture of the Church, be very careful. There are various viewpoints about this subject, and some people are very dogmatic and argumentative about this subject. Again, you may want to talk to the pastor about this subject before you preach on it.

Be punctual in ending your meetings when the pastor gives you a time limit. Obey the pastor of the church while you are there. Your purpose for being there is to help build the pastor's vision. If you did not finish what you felt the Lord wanted you to do because of time constraints given by the pastor, you will not have to answer to the Lord about that. Since the pastor is in charge, he is responsible to the Lord for the content that was or wasn't shared.

In a series of meetings, traveling ministers should take the opportunity to be a blessing to the pastor by doing something for him personally. Here are a few suggestions for a traveling minister if he wants to bless a pastor.

1. Buy at least one of the meals when the pastor takes you out to eat.

2. Buy the pastor a gift, especially if you know of an area that he is interested in.

3. Some of your books and tapes may be appreciated by the pastor.

Don't add the names of the church people to your mailing list without asking the pastor first. Some traveling ministers use the church directory to add the names of the people in the church to their mailing list, even if they do not have permission to do so. This is certainly unethical and should be avoided by every traveling minister.

Again, always ask to see a copy of your hotel bill before you leave to see that only the proper charges are on it, even if the church is paying for it. You can avoid a lot of potential misunderstandings or accusations by making sure that everything on your hotel bill is accurate. Let's review some "no-no's" when staying at a hotel:

1. Do not leave any telephone calls on the hotel bill.
2. Do not put any laundry charges on the hotel bill.
3. Do not put any food on the hotel bill unless previous arrangements have been made with the church.
4. Do not put TV pay channel or movie charges on your hotel bill.

If a member of the local congregation attends your book and tape table, you might consider paying him or giving him something from your table as a gesture of your appreciation. You should not expect people to do this without compensation.

Personal Notes

Personal Notes

You may want to ask the pastor to give you names of pastor friends in the area to call about scheduling a meeting in their church. Some pastors do not want to give you any names of their friends, so be sensitive to their desires. As a general rule, you may only want to ask this of pastors with whom you have a good relationship.

It is acceptable to call the ministers the pastor refers and say to them, "Pastor So-and-so had me in for a meeting, and he suggested that I give you a call to see if you might be interested in receiving some ministry information or scheduling a meeting."

ETHICAL CONDUCT TOWARD PEOPLE

See people as God sees them. They are valuable and precious, and God loves them very dearly. Remember that Christ gave His life for each one of them and that God has a plan for every one of them. There are people with great potential in every congregation, and you have the great privilege of adding to their lives from the revelation of the Word of God and by the anointing of the Holy Spirit.

Do not take people for granted. People can help determine how the Holy Spirit moves and ministers in the meetings. As the people desire to receive from the ministry of the Word and from the Holy Spirit, you as a minister can move in greater anointing and power. Often, effective and successful ministry is the cooperative effort of both the minister and the people in the congregation. Be appreciative toward the people, showing your gratitude for their attendance, attentiveness, and receptivity.

Be personable and accessible to the people. Follow Jesus' example of being available to the people. Be willing to take time to minister to people, so they can see how much God Himself wants to spend time with them. As a representative of God, we should let the nature and character of God show through us. This gives hope to other people when they see that God has done a redemptive work in you.

Do not single out "money people" for financial reasons. Ministers must determine never to be "bought" with money. Do not let the devil manipulate you by dangling money in front of you. Resist the idea that by doing certain things maybe you will cause a certain person to give you money. God is big enough to take care of you, so get your eyes off of people and what they can or cannot do for you. A good rule to follow is to get permission from the pastor before meeting privately with any people from his congregation.

If you have questions about what is ethical in a certain situation, wait until you know what is right before deciding to get involved. If necessary, get some advice from the pastor or call another minister friend for some advice. Your personal integrity is at stake, and you should

Personal Notes

Personal Notes

make every effort to avoid all appearances of evil in every area.

It is interesting to watch the process of excusing unethical behavior. Almost without exception, a minister starts compromising his integrity in small things that really do not matter to others. The problem is that the minister has violated his conscience before God, and if he does not make adjustments, he will soon compromise in areas that will affect other people also.

Make it a goal to see how much you can give to the people. Do not use people for your personal gain. Resist looking at people as a means of getting what you have been "believing for." Make sure your trust is in God, and then let God take care of you as you minister to the people out of a pure heart.

You have been sent to bless people with the Good News of Jesus Christ. Concentrate more on being a blessing than on wondering who is going to bless you.

ADVICE FOR TRAVELING MINISTERS IN THEIR HOME CHURCHES

Realize that a pastor has to spend time with the rest of his church people. Allow the pastor the freedom to take care of his congregation. There will be times when the pastor can fellowship with you, and other times when his schedule is too busy to get together with you. Do not insist on being the pastor's best friend, unless the relationship is mutual.

Cultivate proper relationships with the church people. If some of them give regularly into your ministry, you may want to let your pastor know about it. Your pastor will probably not mind if his people give into your ministry; however, good communication between the pastor and yourself can help avoid a lot of misunderstandings.

Keep your pastor updated on what is happening with your ministry, then he can properly relate to you and get involved with any special projects you may be doing. This allows the pastor to work together with you.

Do not ask your pastor about church details or people in the congregation; that is none of your business. Legally, ministers are to keep all information concerning their church people confidential.

CONCLUSION

Remember the word "ethics" has to do with your character and ideals and also involves principles of right conduct. Make it a primary goal to conduct yourself in a manner so as to reflect the character and glory of God and to be an example to others around you.

Personal Notes

1 TIMOTHY 4:12
... but be thou an example of the believers, in word, in conversation, in charity, in spirit, in faith, in purity.

21

Ethics and the Traveling Minister

PART TWO

It may seem that being a traveling minister thrusts you into a very competitive arena where you have to fight for everything you want. Some traveling ministers point to the fact that there are only so many churches available to minister in as the reason why they begin to view other traveling ministers as competition. As a result of this, some traveling ministers are tempted to be less than ethical toward their fellow ministers.

However, God has a better way of opening doors for traveling ministers than by throwing all traveling ministers into an arena, saying, "May the best person win." God has

Personal Notes

a unique plan for every minister, and no one can actually take the place of another minister. God has deposited certain gifts within ministers, and He will open a door for those gifts to be used. Learn to rest in the gifts of God that are within you, knowing that God is working on your behalf.

AVOID COMPETITION

There is a good kind of competition where you press on and make every effort to complete what God has told you to do. The Apostle Paul concentrated on what God wanted him to do, and he pressed on to the rewards that God had for him.

PHILIPPIANS 3:13,14
Brethren, I count not myself to have apprehended: but this one thing I do, forgetting those things which are behind, and reaching forth unto those things which are before,
I press toward the mark for the prize of the high calling of God in Christ Jesus.

A traveling minister should never compete against another minister. The Apostle Paul finished the course that God instructed him to run. He did not compare himself with others in the ministry.

PROVERBS 18:16
A man's gift maketh room for him, and bringeth him before great men.

2 TIMOTHY 4:7
I have fought a good fight, I have finished MY course, I have kept the faith.

When you compare yourself with other ministers, you measure yourself by a standard that God did not intend for you to use as a measuring stick. If you do this, you will either judge yourself by a standard that you cannot attain to, or you will justify yourself according to something less than God's Word or calling upon your life. As a result, comparison can keep you from fulfilling God's plan for your life.

2 CORINTHIANS 10:12
For we dare not make ourselves of the number, or compare ourselves with some that commend themselves: but they measuring themselves by themselves, and comparing themselves among themselves, are not wise.

There is no excuse for stepping on fellow traveling ministers. God's plan is big enough to keep and sustain you. True faith will let the other minister have what he wants while you believe God and take the rest. The example of Abraham letting Lot choose the land he wanted first reflects the spirit in which fellow ministers ought to act toward each other.

Personal Notes

GENESIS 13:8,9

And Abram said unto Lot, Let there be no strife, I pray thee, between me and thee, and between my herdmen and thy herdmen; for we be brethren.

Is not the whole land before thee? separate thyself, I pray thee, from me: if thou wilt take the left hand, then I will go to the right; or if thou depart to the right hand, then I will go to the left.

PROPER ETHICS AMONG TRAVELING MINISTERS

The following list of issues includes some areas in which traveling ministers need to conduct themselves ethically.

- Never take another traveling minister's meeting dates that have already been scheduled in a church. That is the same as stealing from a fellow minister. Some traveling ministers are convinced that there are not enough churches for all the traveling ministers that need meetings, and they are intent on getting meetings however they can. But again, God's gift will make room for you and create a place for your gift to function.
- Never talk bad about another traveling minister to anyone. Sometimes a bad report or a warning has to be given about a fellow traveling minister, but that should be the exception, not the rule of con-

duct. It's been said that pushing someone else down will not help you climb any higher.

- Never discuss your problems with other traveling ministers, unless a relationship has been developed so that a constructive answer can be reached. Often other traveling ministers have problems of their own. Always try to get advice for your problems from people who can offer a solution or have gone through what you are dealing with.

- Never discuss pastors with other traveling ministers. Unless a person is a pastor they may not understand the motive and reasons why pastors do what they do. Some pastors and traveling ministers may not click because of personality differences. Other ministers may relate their negative experience to you and cause you to have preconceived ideas about the pastor before you ever meet him. How many times have you formed a negative opinion about someone based upon what someone else said, only to discover as you met the person that you get along great?

CONCLUSION

How you treat your fellow traveling ministers may not be apparent to others, but God watches over us all. God will promote you on the basis of what you have

Personal Notes

_____

_____

_____

_____

_____

_____

_____

_____

_____

_____

_____

_____

_____

JOHN 13:34,35
A new commandment I give unto you, That ye love one another; as I have loved you, that ye also love one another. By this shall all men know that ye are my disciples, if ye have love one to another.

Personal Notes

proven trustworthy and faithful with. Learn to adhere to the principles of right conduct as outlined in Scripture.

Endeavor to treat others as you have been treated by Christ. Jesus gave us a new commandment — to love one another as He has loved us. Extend the love of God to your fellow traveling ministers, and you will be blessed by the relationships you are able to build.

A Pastor's Perspective

What do pastors like and dislike? What concerns do pastors have as they pastor the same people on a long-term basis? What motivates pastors to give of themselves continually as they watch over the people that God has entrusted to their care?

These are some of the questions that traveling ministers should think about as they minister in churches. Traveling ministers seldom think about the price that a pastor has paid to have a good church, or the hard work that was necessary for the church to be successful and effective. Much of what it took to cause a church to be

Personal Notes

_____

_____

_____

_____

_____

_____

_____

_____

_____

_____

_____

_____

EPHESIANS 4:1-3
I therefore, the prisoner of the Lord, beseech you that ye walk worthy of the vocation wherewith ye are called,
With all lowliness and meekness, with long-suffering, forbearing one another in love; Endeavouring to keep the unity of the Spirit in the bond of peace.

effective is not apparent or visible to someone who is only at the church for several days.

The primary concern of the traveling minister should be to help the pastor build his church and accomplish his vision. God has placed the pastor in charge of the local church. The vision for the church is given to the pastor so he can lead the congregation into what God desires them to do.

Traveling ministers should never view their ministry separate from the local church. Some traveling ministers go into a local church and their only goal is to promote their own vision. They have no interest in helping the pastor build his church. Because some traveling ministers have shown this type of attitude, there are pastors who feel very negative about having traveling ministers come into their church.

A good traveling minister will always put the local church above his own interests. It is never an option for a traveling minister to come into a church and do his own thing. Remember that touching people with the Good News of Jesus Christ is the chief concern of God, and it should be of highest priority with a traveling minister. When a traveling minister comes to a local church, he should leave it in better condition than it was in before he came.

PASTORAL CONCERNS ABOUT TRAVELING MINISTERS

Here are some concerns that pastors have in working with traveling ministers. Recognizing these issues can help a traveling minister relate properly to the pastoral ministry.

- Pastors are concerned that developing friendships with traveling ministers may create a pressure to have them minister at their church. Traveling ministers should clearly communicate that this is not the reason for their friendship.

- Traveling ministers should not act "super-spiritual." You should be yourself. Being friendly and touchable will help people receive from you.

- Do not come into a church demanding your own way. Flow with the pastor's vision and the way he does things in the church.

- Some traveling ministers mention from the pulpit their hopes of the pastor inviting them back. However, by doing this, they bypass the authority of the pastor. The people then watch to see what the pastor's response will be, and it places unnecessary pressure on the pastor.

- Do not try to schedule another meeting with the pastor right after you have a meeting at his church. The pastor may want to have some time to evaluate the results of the meeting before he decides to invite you back.

- Do not use any of the church's equipment without permission. Be very careful about asking the pastor about using his office equipment or other things in the church to do something that you need to get done. Often the pastor will say you can use his equipment when he really doesn't want you to, simply because he doesn't know what else to say when you ask him.

- Asking for traveling reimbursements is generally a "no-no."

- Do not push your mailing list. Get permission from the pastor before adding his church members to your mailing list.

- Refrain from talking to the pastor about the way you were treated by another pastor. That does not create good will between you and the pastor.

- It is important for traveling ministers to be accountable to someone. The following is a list of people to whom a traveling minister could make himself accountable.

    1. His pastor
    2. His home church
    3. A Board of Directors
    4. A ministerial organization with whom he is licensed or ordained

5. A CPA or someone who is knowledgeable in business and finance

6. The pastor in whose church he is ministering

- Always express your gratitude. Be sure to send thank-you letters. Holding a meeting without sending a thank-you letter to the pastor communicates how little you valued that meeting.

- Do your best to answer all personal correspondence you receive. Remember that a letter unanswered for more than ten days sends a negative message to the individual as to what you think of him and his correspondence.

- You may want to tell the pastor what you desire to do between meetings, especially if the pastor asks you. Some pastors will want to spend a lot of time with you and others do not want to spend any time with you at all.

    1. Do you want to be entertained or go sightseeing?

    2. Do you want to play sports?

    3. Do you want to be alone?

    4. Do you want to go shopping?

    5. Are there certain things that you need or want to accomplish?

- Some traveling ministers, especially lady ministers, have a traveling companion with them, because it

Personal Notes

is safer and more comfortable for two people to travel together. If you have a traveling companion with you, make sure you communicate that to the pastor when the meeting is being scheduled, so the pastor can prepare properly for both of you.

> **TIP:** Be very careful about taking someone with you, because this usually creates an extra expense for the church. If you sense that this is a burden to the church, you may want to offer to take care of your traveling companion's expenses while you are ministering at the church.

- Guard your tongue when you are talking to other people, so you will only share things that are edifying. Do your best to refrain from telling the pastor all the latest gossip that is going around. You will get a reputation, and that type of reputation does not help you as a traveling minister, because the pastor may feel as though he can't share anything with you in confidence.
- If you have books and tapes, communicate this information in advance so the church can prepare a table for them. If you have books or tapes of other ministries you should get the pastor's approval prior to bringing or setting up your book table. Some pastors simply do not want you to

bring any books and tapes into their church. Find out what they want and flow with it.

- If you are going to different churches in the same city, communicate with the pastors in that city where you have already been. Some traveling ministers have a policy that if they have already been in one church in a town or city they do not accept invitations from other churches in the same town. The only exception would be if the pastor where you have already ministered has set up the other meetings. Do your best to avoid creating strife between pastors.

- Spend some time fellowshipping with the pastor. Often you are sent there to minister to the pastor as much as to the people. Pastors are lonely because they do not have anyone they can talk to about the things they are going through. Do what you can to encourage and build up the pastor while you are ministering at his church.

DEALING WITH THE WORD OF GOD

Realize that pastors give a lot of practical teaching. Be careful not to make them appear unspiritual. If you're not careful, people might think negatively of the pastor after you leave. You need to always build up the pastor in the eyes of his people.

Personal Notes

Preach the simple Gospel of Christ. Believe that the Word you preach will confirm what the pastor has been saying. Pastors don't want a mess to clean up afterward. Here is a list of some things to stay away from when you are preaching.

1. Stay away from deep, complicated revelations.
2. Do not major on controversial subjects.
3. Do not tell ethnic jokes.
4. Do not preach your opinions or preferences.
5. Do not try to correct everything that is wrong in the church.

DEALING WITH ACCOMMODATIONS

Complaining about your accommodations is a definite "no-no"! Even if they are not the best, keep your mouth shut and stay in faith. God will give you the grace that is necessary so that you can stay where your host puts you.

Be conservative when you order your food from the menu, especially when the pastor is paying for it. Follow the pastor's example, and order something that is similar in price.

Sometimes when there is no hotel in the area, or the church cannot afford to pay for a hotel, the pastor will inform you that he has made arrangements for you to stay at someone's house. Here are some guidelines when you are staying in someone's home:

1. Do your best to eat what is put in front of you.
2. Always clean up after yourself, especially in the bathroom.
3. Be observant and respect other peoples' schedules.
4. Never be in the house alone with a member of the opposite sex, including the pastor's wife. Always try to avoid any potentially dangerous moments of temptation.
5. Always talk positively about the local church and the pastor to the people with whom you are staying.

DEALING WITH THE CONGREGATION

- Refuse to counsel members of the congregation, unless the pastor requests that you do so. It is not really your job to take care of the congregation's problems, and depending upon what the problems are, it may not even be any of your business.
- Treat people who are apparently wealthy the same as you would any other person. Do not try to get close to "money people" in the congregation so that you might get some of their money. You do not have to resort to questionable means of getting money because God is big enough to supply all of your needs.

Personal Notes

Personal Notes

_____

_____

_____

_____

_____

_____

_____

_____

_____

_____

_____

_____

_____

_____

_____

_____

_____

- Avoid putting successful businessmen from other churches on your ministry board without prior permission from their pastor. Their pastor may be able to share with you some things about them that you don't know, thereby saving you a lot of potential grief.

- If you have to contact church people to do business with them, let the pastor know that you are contacting them. Always remember that good communication with the pastor will help keep your relationship intact.

- Do not make radical claims that your ministry will dramatically change people overnight. You will have to live up to your advertising and do what you said. Otherwise you can be accused of false advertising.

- Always be courteous with all of the church staff, volunteers, and especially the church secretary. If you build a good relationship with the church staff and secretary, they will help you accomplish effective ministry while you are there.

- Exercise caution in listening too much to the associate pastor. Watch out for strife, differing viewpoints, or other existing problems between the associate and the senior pastor. Avoid getting in the middle of these arguments or problems as much as possible. If the senior pastor insists that you get involved, always do your best to remain scriptural, encourage the associate pastor to walk in love and respect the senior pastor, and try to do what you can to help and promote the senior pastor.

CONCLUSION

People will talk about how you treat pastors and the people in the congregation. Therefore, let others talk about your goodness, instead of giving them something bad to talk about. You can do this by endeavoring to walk worthy of the calling of God upon your life.

Personal Notes

23

Proper Ethics in Fund-Raising

As a traveling minister, you will probably find yourself involved in some form of fund-raising at some time or another. It may be for monthly support, a missions trip, or a piece of equipment you need. God has ordained that money is to be used in preaching the Gospel of Jesus Christ. Money is not evil in itself — it is how you deal with money that you have to be concerned about.

Traveling ministers need to trust God at all times for their finances, no matter what method they use to raise the funds. They must also be careful not to compromise

_____

_____

_____

_____

_____

_____

_____

_____

_____

_____

_____

_____

1 TIMOTHY 6:10,11
For the love of money is the root of all evil: which while some coveted after, they have erred from the faith, and pierced themselves through with many sorrows.

But thou, O man of God, flee these things; and follow after righteousness, godliness, faith, love, patience, meekness.

their ethics and integrity by using questionable means to obtain money.

Have you ever seen a ministry that was raising money for some project, and it was obvious that their motives and even their methods were unscriptural, or at least questionable? When something like that is observed, it makes people very cautious about being involved. While people may give some money for a short period of time, it hinders the relationship that could have been developed over a long period of time.

GOD'S PERSPECTIVE

What do you believe God wants for you and your traveling ministry? Do you think He wants you to struggle and barely get by? Do believe that He will supply your basic needs but not your wants or desires? Or are you convinced that God is your Source and that He wants you and your ministry to operate in His abundance according to His riches through Christ Jesus?

God wants you to have more than enough money to operate your traveling ministry. But He will meet you on the level that you trust Him. If you only trust God to barely get by, then that is all you will have. If you believe God will only supply your basic needs with nothing left over, God will do that for you. However, God's abundant blessings will come to you if you are fully persuaded that God's abundance is His will for you and your ministry.

You must develop a strong trust in God that no matter what your needs are, or what project God has assigned to you, He has more than enough to provide for you.

Look at the example of Jesus. In all of His travels, He never lacked for anything. If Jesus did not have enough resources in the natural, the supernatural power of God supplied what was needed. Let's look at the instances where God's abundant supply was more than enough for Jesus and His needs, current projects, and ministry.

1. Jesus received finances from other people to take care of His ministry and the disciples that were traveling with him (Luke 8:3).

2. Jesus' ministry team had enough money with them to buy food in the village in Samaria (John 4:8).

3. Jesus was able to feed the multitudes with the supernatural multiplication of the food they already had in hand (Luke 9:10-17).

4. Jesus was able to pay His taxes by the supernatural direction of God telling Him where the necessary finances were (Matthew 17:24-27).

5. If Jesus did not have what He needed, He knew where to find it. For example, He knew where there was a donkey available when He needed it (Mark 11:2-7). And He also knew where a room was available so that He and His disciples could celebrate the Passover meal (Luke 22:10-13).

Personal Notes

ROMANS 8:32

He that spared not his own Son, but delivered him up for us all, how shall he not with him also freely give us all things?

Personal Notes

_____

_____

_____

_____

_____

_____

_____

_____

_____

_____

_____

_____

_____

_____

_____

_____

If God supplied whatever Jesus needed in His earthly ministry, He will also supply abundantly for your ministry. God has more than enough for you, and He knows how to get what you need to you. God will arrange divine appointments and cause divine transactions to take place if you will trust Him and make Him your Source.

WHY DO YOU WANT TO RAISE MONEY?

Your attitude is the most important factor in fund-raising. You attitude toward God and money will greatly determine whether God will help you get the money you need. Zig Ziglar states that sometimes people need a "checkup from the neck up." Check yourself by asking the following questions to determine whether or not your attitudes are correct.

1. Is your desire to build the Kingdom of God, or is it to get as much as possible for yourself?
2. Are you personally willing to give first before you ask others to give?
3. Can you trust God while you are using a particular program to raise funds? If not, it may be wise to wait until you can.
4. Does money have its proper place in your life?
5. Are you just using people and their money to build your ministry? Or are people your ministry, and fund-raising a side issue?

Your inner motive, or intent, for raising money is also very important.

1. What are you going to use the money for?
2. Is this project God's direction for you or something you want to do?
3. You cannot expect God to answer your request if you ask with the wrong motive, or if it is not the will of God for you.

1 TIMOTHY 6:10
For the love of money is the root of all evil: which while some coveted after, they have erred from the faith, and pierced themselves through with many sorrows.

JAMES 4:3
Ye ask, and receive not, because ye ask amiss, that ye may consume it upon your lusts.

THINGS TO AVOID IN FUND-RAISING

Multi Level Marketing plans (MLM's) may not be wrong in themselves, but many people cannot separate the good intentions you have in helping someone through MLM's from the fact that you are actually asking for money up front. As a traveling minister, you may be approached by multi-level marketing companies telling

Personal Notes

Personal Notes

you that as you travel you can make a lot of money by presenting their company as you go from church to church.

Although there are legitimate MLM's out there, many prey upon a person's desire to get rich quickly or to get something without working for it. If you decide to get involved in a multi-level marketing company, you may want to consider the following guidelines:

1. How long has the company been in business? Choose a company that is not a fly-by-night company. Choose one that has been in business long enough to establish a reputable track record.

2. What kind of people own the company? Investigate the people who started the company to see how ethical and experienced they are.

3. How reputable and dependable is the company with its payments? Check to see if the company is dependable in making its payments to its distributors and salespeople.

4. Does the company focus on selling products or on building a "downline"? Reputable companies will emphasize their products rather than just trying to sign up a number of people who each have to pay a fee for getting into the company.

5. Is the company telling you that you will make an unbelievable amount of money? Avoid getting involved in a multi-level marketing company

because you want to get rich quick. People who get in these types of ventures seldom make a lot of money. Usually the people who get in on the ground level are the only ones who make large amounts of money.

6. Are the people in the company "spiritualizing" their company or business methods? Avoid companies who prey on people with Christian values by trying to show how scriptural their business is, or by trying to tell you that Jesus formed a multi-level marketing company with His disciples to spread the Gospel. If they have to continually justify their company and methods by referring to Scripture, you may need to use great caution before you get involved. Always investigate the companies thoroughly by checking with the Better Business Bureau or by asking other people who have already been involved with the company for a period of time.

Fund-raising gimmicks are a "no-no." If God is really in something, you do not have to resort to some trickster methods or gimmicks to get people's money. Stay away from outlandish claims of special powers or benefits from objects, relics, or things from the Holy Land, and beware of requiring people to do certain acts that aren't scriptural when fund-raising for your ministry.

Personal Notes

JAMES 1:5
If any lack wisdom, let him ask of God, that giveth to all men liberally, and upbraideth not; and it shall be given him.

Chain letters are not only a rip-off, but according to U.S. postal codes they are illegal. These type of letters have been designed to prey on people who are naïve or gullible. Refrain from getting involved with them.

Avoid companies with an undependable reputation in delivering merchandise. When they do not deliver your merchandise as you had promised, your reputation is at stake as much as the company's is. Your customers are going to come to you for the merchandise they ordered.

It is not ethical to prophesy to people about giving money to your ministry. At best that is spiritual manipulation. Various traveling ministers have gotten a bad reputation by doing this. Prophesying to people to give you money is a violation of Scripture.

Paul wrote to the Corinthians and instructed them to give willingly from a cheerful heart, not because someone prophesied to them.

2 CORINTHIANS 9:7
Every man according as he purposeth in his heart, so let him give; not grudgingly, or of necessity: for God loveth a cheerful giver.

Always check with an attorney if you have questions about the legalities of certain fund-raising methods, or if you have questions about becoming involved with certain companies. It is better to investigate ahead of time than to be involved, even innocently, in questionable or uneth-ical fund-raising methods.

THINGS TO CONSIDER IN FUND-RAISING

- Allow plenty of pre-campaign planning time. The fund-raising campaign is not the time to figure out answers to problems or work through a crisis. Taking time to brainstorm with other people and to carefully develop a strategy of what you're going to do can help increase the revenue that you receive.
- Surround yourself with people who are knowl-edgeable of or have had previous experience with the fund-raising methods you are going to use. Their experience can save you a lot of headaches and help you achieve maximum results with your fund-raising.
- Be sure your method of fund-raising will bring in enough funds for the project. Every fund-raising method has limits on how much income it can bring in. Investigate a number of fund-raising methods to see which method is best for your specific project.
- Make sure you are honest in the method of fund-raising you use and in how you conduct yourself.

Personal Notes

Personal Notes

_____

_____

_____

_____

_____

_____

_____

_____

_____

_____

_____

_____

_____

_____

_____

_____

_____

JAMES 1:5
If any of you lack wisdom, let him ask of God, that giveth to all men liberally, and upbraideth not; and it shall be given him.

Always keep your word and deliver what you promised to your customers. Be up front with people about what you are trying to do, and do not misrepresent what you are raising the money for. You should also check to make sure that you are not breaking any state or local laws by your fund-raising methods.

- Avoid all appearance of evil in fund-raising. Some methods may not be a good choice for a ministry to be involved in, even though there is nothing wrong with the methods themselves. If people perceive the methods are wrong, it will give them the wrong impression about your ministry.

- Ask God for His wisdom as you look for a specific fund-raising idea. Seek God until you receive wisdom from Him. Trust in Him and work the idea — then you will see the success you desire.

CONCLUSION

People are sensitive about money issues. Be very clear and specific when communicating about money and about any fund-raising you are doing. Stay with the facts, and be up front with people about what you plan to do with the money. Make sure your fund-raising and accounting methods avoid all appearances of evil and reflect the glory of God.

Developing Your Traveling Ministry

24

Traveling for a Season — Or a Lifetime?

God has a plan for every person. Usually that plan is unfolded or revealed one step at a time. There are various seasons that a person must go through in order to fulfill the plan and purpose of God, just as a plant has to go through various seasons until it finally bears fruit.

Part of the reason that people have to go through seasons or stages is because they must prepare, develop, and train in order to be able to complete the plan and purpose of God. In each season or stage, a person can learn valuable lessons and accomplish something for God.

ECCLESIASTES 3:1

To every thing there is a season, and a time to every purpose under the heaven.

WHAT IS YOUR REAL CALLING?

What I term your "real calling from God" is the ultimate plan and goal God has for you. That is what you are
being prepared for. But often it takes time to actually function and operate in that calling. God guides us through various circumstances and places toward that calling.

Often when a person gets into some kind of ministry,
he thinks he has arrived in the calling God put on his life.
However, God's plan for each individual is a spiritual
journey that unfolds on a road that God has designed. A
person will usually travel along that road during his entire
lifetime.

Look at the original direction you received from
God. Often the ultimate plan and purpose for your life is
revealed there. Take some time to recall that moment
when God revealed His plan and call to you. What did God
share with you at that time?

THE TRAVELING MINISTRY —
FOR TRAINING OR TO FULFILL
THE CALL OF GOD?

God uses various things to train people to do His will.
Every step of the journey that God takes you on is valuable.
Sometimes a person may question how God could ever
receive any glory out of his present situation, or wonder
how his current circumstances could have anything to do

with the plan and call of God for his life. However, God does not waste anything.

Do not be alarmed if you go through several stages of ministry, especially during the early years. Rev. Kenneth E. Hagin maintains that every traveling minister ought to pastor for awhile, and every pastor ought to be in the traveling ministry for awhile.

God has different plans for traveling ministers. Some traveling ministers have not been involved in anything but the traveling ministry, and it seems as if that is all God wants them to do. Others are only in the traveling ministry for a season, and then God tells them to do something else. Still others are primarily involved in some type of pastoral ministry, yet they will occasionally travel to preach elsewhere.

The important thing is that you do not compare yourself with others. There is no absolute rule in the Scriptures that states you have to stay in one area of ministry for your entire life. God uses people in different ways to accomplish His plans.

SCRIPTURAL KEYS TO LONGEVITY

Proper preparation is necessary in order to be in a position long-term. Preparation may not always be easy, especially if a person is not sure about the will of God for his life. It's been said that a person should be prepared to

PSALM 37:23
The steps of a good man are ordered by the Lord: and he delighteth in his way.

1 CORINTHIANS 12:18
But now hath God set the members every one of them in the body, as it hath pleased him.

Personal Notes

_____

_____

_____

_____

_____

_____

_____

_____

_____

_____

_____

_____

_____

move with God at a moment's notice, but plan as if he will stay where he is for a lifetime. In other words, a person should be flexible to move with the direction of God, yet stable enough not to move unless God speaks to him about doing so.

Here are some keys to staying in the traveling ministry on a long-term basis. First, look at the original direction you received from the Lord. Concentrate on the purpose He revealed to you. If your purpose is nothing more than taking care of you and your family, my advice to you is to go seek God again. You must have a greater goal to accomplish than just having a full itinerary of meetings in which to preach, if you want to travel for a long period of time and accomplish something significant for God.

Get a vision from God that is bigger than just meeting your needs. God wants to do more in your life than just meet your needs. How much God can use you is determined by your vision and plans for ministry. During times of prayer begin to ask God to give you a vision to reach many people with the Gospel of Jesus Christ. Stay in the Presence of God until your vision from God is so big that it will take the hand of God to accomplish it.

Get involved in accomplishing something that's bigger than you are. This will give you purpose in what you are doing. Other people's spiritual destinies depend on you being the vessel God wants you to be. Make it a goal to help as many people as you can. Let your plans and your projects reflect your efforts to reach as many people as you can.

Think in terms of meeting goals in the future, rather than just living for the immediate present. Plan ahead to accomplish what God wants you to do. Ministers who only live for today generally are in no position to ever do more than they're doing today. A prudent person looks ahead and prepares himself by setting goals for accomplishing things tomorrow. Whether you are to be in the traveling ministry for a season or for a lifetime, thinking ahead is a must.

Learn to be content in whatever season you are in. Learn every lesson that you can in the season you are currently in. Every season or stage in your life and ministry can contribute to the ultimate plan that God has for your life. How you deal with the lessons in these various seasons will greatly determine how well you accomplish the purpose God has for your life. The Apostle Paul said in Philippians 4:11 that he had learned in whatsoever state he was in, therewith to be content.

Find a need in humanity and fill it. Get involved with making your world a better place in live. If you have a mandate from God's Word to do something, such as to share the Gospel with people, then you don't need to pray about it, asking if it's God's will for you to do it. When you

Personal Notes

PSALM 37:23
The steps of a good man are ordered by the Lord: and he delighteth in his way.

have permission from God's Word to do something, go ahead and do it unless the Spirit of God specifically directs you not to. The Apostle Paul always assumed God was going to let him preach the Gospel wherever he wanted to go, so Paul made preparations to go and went. The only time he didn't go was when the Spirit of God specifically forbade him.

ACTS 16:6-10
Now when they had gone throughout Phrygia and the region of Galatia, and were forbidden of the Holy Ghost to preach the word in Asia,
After they were come to Mysia, they assayed to go into Bithynia: but the Spirit suffered them not.
And they passing by Mysia came down to Troas.
And a vision appeared to Paul in the night; There stood a man of Macedonia, and prayed him, saying, Come over into Macedonia, and help us.
And after he had seen the vision, immediately we endeavoured to go into Macedonia, assuredly gathering that the Lord had called us for to preach the gospel unto them.

Refuse to be moved out of what God led you to do until God tells you it is time to do something different. Resist the pressure of moving when there is a lack of money. Learn to endure hardness as a good soldier. And don't let yourself be manipulated by money when someone offers you a lot of money to do something different. Let God guide you at His pace to the calling He has for you.

Preparing for tomorrow:

1. Remember the original word and direction you received from God. That will help you to know where God wants you to be tomorrow.

2. Train yourself to think and plan long-term. Focus on tomorrow, not just on your immediate circumstances and needs.

3. Prepare wisely with your finances by allocating a portion of your ministry income for future projects. Make a goal to save a portion of your income and put it in a savings account for the future.

4. Develop relationships and friendships with other people. You will need friends so that you can make it through the difficult times. At times you may also need friends to encourage you as you endeavor to do the will of God.

5. Observe and evaluate ministers who operate in the areas of ministry that you are headed toward. Identify role models who have already successful navigated the path you are traveling, then study their life and ministry. Learn the biblical principles they used as they progressed in the will of God. Examine the relationship they maintained with God and their commitment to accomplish God's will. Setting your sights on the right role models will often determine how far you get in ministry.

Personal Notes

Personal Notes

That is one reason why the Apostle Paul said to follow him as he followed Christ.

1 CORINTHIANS 11:1
Be ye followers of me, even as I also am of Christ.

CONCLUSION

William Carey, the father of modern missions had a motto that he followed: "Expect great things from God; attempt great things for God." Keep pressing ahead to do what you are doing now until God tells you otherwise. Assume you have a "green light" from God unless a red light, so to speak, appears in your spirit. Accomplish all that God has destined you to accomplish!

25

Going From Glory To Glory

As in every occupation, there are various levels within the traveling ministry. Every traveling minister is at a different place of growth and development in his ministry. However, there are four general levels of the traveling ministry that can be easily identified.

1. At the first level of traveling ministry, there are those who are just beginning in the traveling ministry — those trying to establish relationships with pastors and schedule meetings. These traveling ministers are probably bi-vocational to supplement the income they receive from the traveling

Personal Notes

_____

_____

_____

_____

_____

_____

_____

_____

_____

_____

_____

_____

_____

_____

_____

PSALM 75:6,7
For promotion cometh neither from the east, nor from the west, nor from the south.
But God is the judge: he putteth down one, and setteth up another.

ministry. Their product table is probably not very developed in quantity or quality. Most of them have no staff to take care of their office. Some may not even have an office, unless it is in their home. Traveling ministers in this category typically include those in their first five years of the traveling ministry.

2. At the second level of traveling ministry, there are those who have been in the traveling ministry for several years but are still not fully established. Typically they travel and minister only in certain regions where they are known, not nationwide. They have established relationships with a number of pastors. They have some meetings, but do not necessarily have a full itinerary. A percentage of this category is probably still bi-vocational. A few of these traveling ministers have an office with staff personnel to take care of administrative needs. Their product table probably includes various items of better quality than that of those in the first category of ministry. They probably have been traveling a minimum of three years.

3. The third level of traveling ministry consists of those who have been established in the traveling ministry for a number of years. Those in this category are generally known nationwide and

perhaps in certain countries abroad. They may have an office located in an office building with various staff personnel depending upon their needs and the projects they are involved in. Scheduling meetings is not a problem for these ministers. Their itinerary is generally full, and they may even have a waiting list. Typically their product table will offer a variety of up-to-date items with full color covers. Some may also offer books, videos, music tapes or CDs, as well as audio products.

4. The fourth level of traveling ministers are those who are well-established and their ministries are known nationally and internationally. These would include the mega-ministries that may even have a radio or television ministry, huge humanitarian aid projects, extensive missions efforts in foreign countries, and possibly even their own network of ministers. They probably have a vast array of products to offer such as videos, audiotape series, music tapes or CDs, books, ministry logo items, and other related material. Some may have authored books that are published through a national publisher. These ministries have a number of people working for them and probably have their own office building or complex.

Personal Notes

IDENTIFY YOUR PRESENT LEVEL
IN THE TRAVELING MINISTRY

These four categories represent the journey, or path, that is possible for traveling ministers. As you read through the four categories of traveling ministries previously listed, you may easily determine at which level your ministry is currently located.

Not all traveling ministries will reach the fourth category because that may not be the will of God for them, or they may not have developed enough to handle that size of ministry.

No matter what your current level, remember to concentrate on personal growth rather than on just growing your ministry. You cannot successfully grow an organization or ministry unless you, as the leader, are willing to grow personally.

Realize that your present level in the traveling ministry is not a life sentence. In other words, it is not necessarily the will of God for you forever. Each day should be another step in progressing more and more in the will of God.

Promotion comes from God. He moves upon people to recognize your gifts when they are properly developed and when you have learned to function effectively in them. It is possible for you to promote yourself by doing certain things. However, be careful that you do not promote yourself into something that you cannot function in effectively, or into something that takes more commitment than you realized.

Let God promote you as you develop and grow in the knowledge of His grace and ability. If you know certain things or methods that you can use to promote your ministry, learn to wait until the Lord tells you to use them. When God tells you to use a certain promotional method, it will benefit your ministry, and it will be a blessing to everyone involved. Learn to trust in God's ability to open doors of utterance for you and give you favor with others in the ministry.

PSALM 75:6,7
For promotion cometh neither from the east, nor from the west, nor from the south.
But God is the judge: he putteth down one, and setteth up another.

KEYS TO INCREASING IN
THE TRAVELING MINISTRY

Once you have identified your level of ministry, you may want to move from one level to the next. Here are some things to consider when preparing to move to the next level.

Put the Word of God in you. You will only rise as high as the material that you feed on. Having the Word of God in you will help you to fulfill all of the will of God for

Personal Notes

your life. As you keep feasting on the Word of God, it becomes a part of you. This will help you to have faith, give you revelation, and give you something meaningful, effective, and powerful to minister to others.

Prayer time with God will give you specific direction. In prayer, God can reveal certain things for you to do that will bring great blessing to many people and also be a blessing to you. During prayer, you can determine whether God is telling you to do something, or if He is wanting someone else to do it. In prayer, you can distinguish between the will of God and personal ambition. Personal dreams will die and God's dreams will be born in you. Never underestimate the value of spending time in prayer. Divine encounters give divine insight, which bring supernatural results!

Value every experience in life. Learn all you can from everything you go through. In some circumstances you will learn what not to do. In other situations you will learn to do some things that will help you in future ministry. Remember, God never wastes anything. Every step of your Christian journey is valuable and can contribute to the value of our ministry. As you learn from your experiences in obeying God, your experience will give you wisdom and credibility in what you say.

Develop relationships continually with other ministers. Effective ministry depends upon relationships that you have developed with God and others. Your traveling ministry will expand largely in proportion to the contacts you have and in proportion to the relationships you have with other ministers. The demand for your ministry will increase as God uses you to touch the lives of other people.

Some traveling ministers do not think that a relationship with other ministers is important as long as they can have a meeting in a church. However, the Scriptures clearly indicate that God thinks relationships are important. God sent His Son to die for the world so that He might have a relationship with mankind. God sent the Holy Spirit to live in us so that He could maintain a relationship with born-again believers.

Believe for favor with every person you cross paths with. Having favor with other people is not an accident. As you walk in the favor of God, He will also give you favor with men. One of the best ways to have the favor of God is to walk in the truth of His Word. As you honor His Word, God will give you favor and cause you to increase.

God's favor and His will work together. When you are walking in God's will, He will grant His favor to shine upon you. People may be lined up to tell you that you should not be in a certain position of ministry and that you are not qualified enough, but God is still more than enough.

Personal Notes

Personal Notes

_____

_____

_____

_____

_____

_____

_____

_____

_____

_____

_____

_____

_____

_____

"You will not change until you are willing to spend money to change your mind. Most people spend more money on their cars than they do on their minds. That is why their cars run better than their minds do."

Bob Harrison

PERSONAL GROWTH LEADS TO INCREASE

Increase will also come in proportion to the change that occurs within you. Change will happen on the inside of you largely through three things:

1. **What you eat.** This can also be referred to as your "spiritual and mental diet." It includes feeding on the Word of God in your daily devotional reading or by listening to audio teaching tapes and videos. It also includes any other books or reading material that you feed upon. Where you are in life and ministry today is greatly determined by what you have fed upon in the past.

2. **Who you associate with.** Your friends and the people you are constantly around can influence you to rise to great things or hinder you so that you never fulfill the will of God. You cannot hang around people who are not interested in doing great things for God, and then go accomplish something significant for God yourself. Learn to properly evaluate the people around you to see if they have the same beliefs and values that you have. Do they display the attitudes and beliefs about the Word of God, the call of God, and about ministry that are necessary to be a successful minister?

3. **What your environment is.** A person's environment will often have an influence upon what a person thinks is acceptable or possible. The place you live, your hangouts, the places you shop, your church, your job, etc. are all elements of a composite environment that help determine the way you think and the actions you take.

God may have spoken to you about being a traveling minister. However, the influence of these three areas can either help you or hinder you in obeying God. Constantly evaluating what you are feeding on, who you are with, and where you are will enable you to maximize your personal growth with God and will prepare you for increase in your traveling ministry.

When you become the kind of person that God wants you to be, your ministry will not be a problem or a struggle. When you change within, your level of ministry will also change. You will be able to resist the temptations of the enemy more, walk according to the Word of God more, and minister under the anointing more effectively.

Look at the example of Jesus. He became the kind of person the Father wanted Him to be, therefore ministry was not a problem for Him. Luke 2:52 tells us that Jesus "increased in wisdom and stature, and in favour with God and man" in the first thirty years of His life. Jesus took time to become the right kind of person so that He could

Personal Notes

Personal Notes

successfully accomplish three years of ministry. Jesus was able to minister effectively to all who received Him. Because Jesus was ready and able, He did not have to refuse anyone's request for ministry.

Many people do not recognize the value of becoming the right kind of person. They do not realize the importance of personal growth. Therefore, they struggle with their ministry and stay far below the level where God wants them to be.

CONCLUSION

God wants to promote you in your traveling ministry. When you change, prepare, and walk through some things, you will have a message, a ministry, and increase. God will cause opportunities and promotion to come your way, and you will literally be able to go from glory to glory — both within yourself and in your ministry!

26

Pitfalls To Avoid in The Traveling Ministry

This lesson outlines a list of things the devil may try to use against you as a traveling minister to derail you and keep you from doing what God said to do. One minister said, "Dreams crash daily on the rocks of temptation…. Ask Samson, and he will tell you that one night of pleasure is not worth a lifetime of blindness."

Because of the nature of the traveling ministry, you may experience a different set of problems, challenges, and temptations than most people do. It would be wise to know what these are, and then to prepare yourself so that the enemy cannot take advantage of you in these

_____

_____

_____

_____

_____

_____

_____

_____

_____

_____

_____

_____

_____

_____

_____

"Dreams crash daily on the rocks of temptation. Move the ship of your life away from those rocks. Ask Samson, and he will tell you, 'One night of pleasure is not worth a lifetime of blindness.'"

Mike Murdock

areas. This lesson does not give an exhaustive list, but it will help you not to be ignorant of some of Satan's devices.

DO NOT NEGLECT YOUR DEVOTION TIME

As a traveling minister, you move continually from place to place, and because your schedule is not always the same, you will be tempted to neglect your devotion time with God. However, that is your personal time with God. Do not allow the devil to use circumstances, pressures, schedules, etc. to rob you of the privilege of spending time with God.

A minister who does not have a devotion time with God on a regular basis can get by for a while. If he continues with no devotions, soon he will lose that fresh touch in his message; he'll have no reserve left when a crisis comes along; and eventually, when he goes to minister to someone, the power of God will be nowhere to be found. A minister may think he is getting by without any devotion time, but other people can usually tell when he is not where he should be in the Lord.

As you travel, look for places to have private devotions where you will not be distracted and where you can experience the peace and Presence of God. Jesus gave some instructions about maintaining a devotional time of prayer with God in Matthew 6:6: "But thou, when thou prayest, enter into thy closet, and when thou hast shut thy door, pray to thy Father which is in secret; and thy Father which seeth in secret shall reward thee openly."

In the midst of a constantly changing schedule, you can still maintain your devotional time with God. It is your privilege to have that time with God, and He will reward you richly as you obey Him.

GETTING BEYOND COMPLACENCY

Sometimes traveling ministers will seek God in order to step into the ministry they have been called to, but after they are in it for a while, they no longer seek God the way they did before. After being in the ministry for a while, it is easy for traveling ministers to fall into the trap of depending upon what they know rather than upon God. They no longer seek God about what to preach on, or about the direction of ministry that God would desire in a certain place.

As a traveling minister, you must fight or contend for the relationship that is necessary in order to be an effective minister. Maintain a fervency and a fire within you for God and His will for your life. Guard your heart so that God and His Word remain a priority with you. You will need to do this if you are to rise to the full potential of the call of God upon your life.

Personal Notes

_____

_____

_____

_____

_____

_____

_____

_____

_____

_____

_____

_____

_____

_____

_____

_____

_____

_____

JUDE 1:3

...exhort you that ye should earnestly contend for the faith which was once delivered unto the saints.

REVELATION 2:4,5

Nevertheless I have somewhat against thee, because thou hast left thy first love.

Remember therefore from whence thou art fallen, and repent, and do the first works; or else I will come unto thee quickly, and will remove thy candlestick out of his place, except thou repent.

DO NOT YIELD TO THE LOVE OF MONEY

Traveling ministers will be faced with financial challenges such as having enough money to pay their bills, to pay for a project, to go on a missions trip, or simply having enough money for their family to live on. Desiring money or even praying for money is not wrong, but it is wrong to love money in such a way that getting money is a higher priority than it should be or is a desire that is gone out of control.

1 TIMOTHY 6:10

...the love of money is the root of all evil: which while some coveted after, they have erred from the faith, and pierced themselves through with many sorrows.

Because of these challenges, some traveling ministers become covetous of pastors and churches where they minister. They develop an inordinate affection for money because it represents a means to obtain the things they are lacking or have to continually contend for. A traveling minister must guard against a covetous heart and not get tired of allowing God Himself to be his security. Trusting God for finances is necessary no matter what level of maturity and anointing a person ministers the Word of God.

As a traveling minister, you should do the best that you know how, and there are ways to conduct yourself so that people can see the excellence that is in your ministry. As a result they will give more money in your offering. However, the temptation for some traveling ministers is to do certain unethical things that will bring more money to them.

Never allow money to become a priority with you or a determining factor in deciding where to minister. The Apostle Peter instructed ministers in First Peter 5:2 to "feed the flock of God which is among you, taking the oversight thereof, not by constraint, but willingly; not for filthy lucre, but of a ready mind...." If you will keep your heart right, continue to develop your faith, and use sound financial management principles in operating your ministry, God will supply every need that you may have.

Personal Notes

DEALING SUCCESSFULLY WITH THE OPPOSITE SEX

As a traveling minister, taking precautions in dealing with members of the opposite sex can help you avoid potential embarrassment and help safeguard your marriage and ministry. Decide beforehand how you will respond if you are put in certain situations.

It is a good idea to institute some policies as guidelines for your conduct. Some suggestions include:

- Do not indulge in off-color stories.
- Be careful what you watch on television in the hotel room.
- Avoid any form of pornography.
- Do not get in compromising situations with people of the opposite sex.
- Do not get emotionally involved with people of the opposite sex.
- Do not counsel people of the opposite sex unless you have a third party with you.
- Do not travel in the same vehicle with someone of the opposite sex unless you are with your spouse.

Once a person is involved in a sexual affair with someone, he will never be the same. He will have to deal with thought patterns and emotional issues that he did not have to deal with before. Even though God and his spouse may forgive him, often other ministers or church people do not forget, and that minister may have to live with reproach for the rest of his life.

> **PROVERBS 6:32,33 (NKJV)**
> **Whoever commits adultery with a woman lacks understanding; He who does so destroys his own soul.**
> **Wounds and dishonor he will get, And his reproach will not be wiped away.**

It's been said, "If you keep playing with fire, you are going to get burned." As a traveling minister, you must always be aware of the wiles of the enemy. Using people of the opposite sex to tempt ministers and cause them to fall has been a favorite ploy of the devil for years. Remember that Ephesians 4:27 tells us to give no place to the devil.

OVERCOME THE LUST OF DISTRACTIONS

There are many things that will catch your eye that seem appealing and desirable. Most of those things are sent by the devil as an attempt to choke the Word and distract you from the calling of God in your life until no eternal fruit ever comes forth.

> **MARK 4:18,19**
> **And these are they which are sown among thorns; such as hear the word,**

Personal Notes

Personal Notes

And the cares of this world, and the deceitfulness of riches, and the lusts of other things entering in, choke the word, and it becometh unfruitful.

The question that you as a traveling minister must always ask yourself before you get involved in something is, "Will this help me or hinder me in fulfilling the call of God upon my life?" Fulfilling your ministry hinges upon how you answer that question. Learn to say "no" to things that do not contribute to fulfilling the will of God.

As you determine what you should be involved in, remember what God spoke to you when He called you into the ministry. Some things are not wrong in themselves; however, they become wrong when they hinder you from pursuing the will of God and studying His Word.

RESIST THE GLITTER OF RECOGNITION

Some traveling ministers are in the traveling ministry because of the fame and honor they receive. They receive honor and respect that they would not receive otherwise. However, a traveling minister should remember that he is a servant of God, and he should be quick to give God the glory for any recognition that he receives.

Notice that Philip was mightily used of God to bring revival in Samaria. People were born again, healed, and received miracles in their lives. Philip was the vessel that God used to touch people's lives, but it was actually the power of God that changed their lives. If God's power had not manifested, Philip could have not have accomplished anything.

> **ACTS 8:6,26**
> **And the people with one accord gave heed unto those things which Philip spake, hearing and seeing the miracles which he did....**
> **And the angel of the Lord spake unto Philip, saying, Arise, and go toward the south unto the way that goeth down from Jerusalem unto Gaza, which is desert.**

Later God told Philip to go to the desert. If Philip had been seeking fame and recognition, he would probably not have obeyed God. But he would also have missed the blessing of ministering to the eunuch that he met at the oasis in the desert. To be an effective minister, you must be willing to leave the glitter of recognition and do what God tells you to do. As you obey God, you will be able to experience the true glory of God in your ministry.

AVOID "CANNED SERMONS"

Traveling ministers move from place to place, and because they have a new crowd virtually every week, they can use the same sermons over and over again. Thus the temptation is there for a traveling minister to preach the same sermons repeatedly instead of seeking God's direction for ministry and the specific word that God would have him to preach.

After a while the sermons are not fresh anymore, and the Spirit of God has no opportunity to interact with the minister as he shares the Word of God. Learn to be an able minister that speaks the Word of God as the Spirit directs.

2 CORINTHIANS 3:6
Who also hath made us able ministers of the new testament; not of the letter, but of the spirit: for the letter killeth, but the spirit giveth life.

Devotional time with God is necessary to stay fresh and up-to-date with God. Hearing from God on a daily basis is necessary for successful ministry, and this is often accomplished during a minister's devotional time.

Learn to minister out of the overflow of your personal walk with God. A minister literally has to have the message working in his own life before he can share it with much conviction and power. If the message has no effect upon the minister, it certainly will not contain enough life and anointing to change other people's lives.

RESIST THE PRESSURE TO PERFORM

Although there may be some similarities, every traveling minister is different because of each one's callings and purpose. Some traveling ministers are preachers called primarily to win the lost. Others operate more as teachers and concentrate on the maturing of the saints. Some traveling ministers have a very good music ministry along with their preaching ministry. Others do not have the ability to sing, but they may have authored several books.

God uses ministers in different ways. Some ministers want to do the latest thing that is going around in Christian circles simply because it will draw a lot of people. For example, if God is moving in the area of healing, some ministers will want to begin healing meetings. It would be better for ministers to follow God's plan for their life rather than just following the latest fad.

In some places where you minister the anointing of God may be very strong, and the gifts of the Spirit will manifest to minister to people. In another place the anointing may not be as strong, and although there is no unction of the Spirit to minister with the gifts of the Spirit, the people may be expecting that type of ministry. Thus there will be a pressure to perform and make something happen. However, it is very important to minister by the unction of the Holy Spirit rather than yield to the pressure to perform.

Concentrate on the gifts and callings that God has put in your life and ministry. Be what God called you to be, and you will be successful. Focus on ministering what

Personal Notes

God has revealed to you in the way that the Holy Spirit is directing you to minister. As you obey God's direction you will see the anointing of God increase upon your ministry, and you will be more effective.

> **1 PETER 4:10,11**
> **As every man hath received the gift, even so minister the same one to another, as good stewards of the manifold grace of God.**
> **If any man speak, let him speak as the oracles of God; if any man minister, let him do it as of the ability which God giveth: that God in all things may be glorified through Jesus Christ, to whom be praise and dominion for ever and ever. Amen.**

CONCLUSION

There are many pitfalls and temptations that Satan may try to use against you in the traveling ministry. Satan is your enemy, and you need to know how to deal with the devil and his temptations effectively.

> **EPHESIANS 6:11**
> **Put on the whole armour of God, that ye may be able to stand against the wiles of the devil.**

> **1 PETER 5:8**
> **Be sober, be vigilant; because your adversary the devil, as a roaring lion, walketh about, seeking whom he may devour.**

You should always remember that the Spirit of God on the inside of you is greater than anyone or anything that would confront you. When you are faced with situations and temptations beyond what you can handle, remember that you are a child of God and that you can ask God for His wisdom. James 1:5 promises that God will give it to you willingly and liberally.

1 JOHN 4:4
Ye are of God, little children, and have overcome them: because greater is he that is in you, than he that is in the world.

JAMES 1:5
If any of you lack wisdom, let him ask of God, that giveth to all men liberally, and upbraideth not; and it shall be given him.

Personal Notes

_____

_____

_____

_____

_____

_____

_____

_____

_____

_____

_____

27

Perfecting Your Style

Each person has a starting place in fulfilling his or her calling in the ministry. Some people have a good, well-prepared start, and others have a pretty rocky start. The important thing to know is that you must get started. God cannot perfect a person's ministry if that person is doing nothing, any more than you could steer a parked car. If you are called of God into the traveling ministry, you must get started in order for God to begin to bless you, perfect you, and bring increase to you.

Sometimes I tell people, "Today is the worst you will ever see me, because tomorrow I'll be better!" I can say that with confidence because I know that God is constantly working in my life, and I am willing to let Him do the work that is necessary. God is faithful to do the work in me that is needed. Not everything about me is perfect, but according to God's Word, I am being perfected.

PSALM 138:8 (NKJV)
The Lord will perfect that which concerns me; Your mercy, O Lord, endures forever; Do not forsake the works of Your hands.

Have you ever heard of a pitcher in Major League Baseball throwing a "perfect game" — a game in which no one got any hits or got on base? It is a rare moment in baseball history when that happens. What many don't realize is the amount of time that a pitcher must spend practicing to hone his skills and perfect his style of pitching until he is effective.

This lesson contains some ideas, information, and principles to help you be all that God has called you to be, to help you express that calling effectively and in the best way possible, and to help you perfect your style of ministry.

IDENTIFY YOUR STYLE OF PREACHING AND TEACHING

You are an individual created in the image of God. God wants to express Himself through you, using your personality and uniqueness. God created you with talents, gifts, and strengths that compliment your personality. Concentrate on developing your personality and abilities so that you are an expression of Christ in the earth.

You cannot do everything. Choose specific styles and methods to help you be effective in the ministry. They should reflect your purpose for being in the ministry and should compliment the gifts and talents you already have within you. Study other ministers to see how they do the things you are endeavoring to do.

God will give you a specific ministry as well as a specific message for the Body of Christ. Identify both your ministry and your message. Watch the positions and functions where God anoints you the most — that can be a real clue as to the specific ministry God has given to you. Also note carefully the messages where the anointing flows the strongest. You cannot successfully preach or teach everything, so learn to concentrate on what God has anointed you to say. As you do this, you will find the anointing of God flowing through you stronger than ever, and your ministry will be more effective.

DEVELOPING YOUR OWN STYLE OF MINISTRY

When you first start ministering, you will find yourself copying those who have influenced you greatly or those with whom you have associated closely. As you begin ministering, it may seem as though you are doing things the way someone else does them and that it's difficult to be yourself. However, starting in the ministry is like learning to walk. You learn to walk by holding the hand of someone who can already walk and is willing to reach down to steady and support you. That is also how you begin to minister.

Associating with a seasoned minister who is willing to give you a steadying hand of support is a real key to becoming an effective minister. This will help you grow to the next level and avoid potentially harmful situations, and it will enable the wisdom of God to come forth through you.

Identify role models you would want to emulate; studying these will provide guidance for you as you progress in the ministry. Often the invisible qualities that God wants to work in you are difficult to imagine until you actually see them in someone else. Good role models become a visible picture of what God wants to do in your life.

Over a period of time, your own style of teaching and preaching will come forth as you spend time with God and become secure and able in the call of God upon your life.

STUDY THE SCRIPTURES UNTIL YOU RECEIVE REVELATION FROM THEM

As you study the Scriptures and receive revelation from them, it will allow the power of God to move through you. Truth that has convicted you to live a more godly life will convict others as you share it with them. When truth of God's Word becomes a part of you, the power of God can manifest through you to change people's lives.

Rev. Kenneth E. Hagin's revelation is great, but you have to study the Scriptures to get your own revelation and understanding of them. What you understand from the Scriptures may be the same truth that Brother Hagin knows and understands. However, it must still be revelation to you before you can share it with conviction, anointing, and the power of God.

It is not enough to merely have information in your head or read it from a book. Information is not necessarily something you have embraced as a belief or incorporated into your lifestyle. Therefore it may not be a part of you.

Revelation as referred to in the context of this lesson is the truth that is in your heart, or spirit. Actually what we commonly refer to as revelation is really illumination given by the Holy Spirit concerning the Scriptures. It is the

Personal Notes

process whereby the truth of God's Word is written in the heart of an individual and becomes a part of his being and lifestyle. This kind of revelation, or illumination, is necessary both to live the Christian life successfully and to be an effective minister.

ELEMENTS THAT ARE NECESSARY TO PERFECT YOUR STYLE

1. Realize that it takes time for God to work in your life the things that are revealed in Scripture to you. Brother Hagin advises the students at Rhema Bible Training Center to prove their revelation in their own lives before sharing it from the pulpit. Let time be your ally. Make sure you have a solid understanding of a truth before you share it with others.

   Walk out the truths that you see in Scripture in your own life before you preach them to others. It can save you embarrassment, especially if you only have a partial understanding of the subject, or the supposed truth did not actually bring the desired results in your life.

2. Do not compare yourself with others. Be who you are in Christ. God has made you like no other individual, and He has deposited certain gifts, talents, and strengths in you to accomplish specific assignments. In that sense you are irreplaceable.

There are assignments and projects that only you may be able to accomplish, and there are people to reach with the Gospel that only you may be able to reach. God creates specific times and opportunities for you to accomplish these things.

As you continue in the traveling ministry, you will have opportunity to compare yourself with other traveling ministers. You can never win that game — someone will always preach better than you, have better promotion material, have more income, or have more partners than you do. Remember what Paul said about comparing yourself with others.

2 CORINTHIANS 10:12
For we dare not make ourselves of the number, or compare ourselves with some that commend themselves: but they measuring themselves by themselves, and comparing themselves among themselves, are not wise.

As you fulfill your ministry, you are on a specific course ordained by God. You are called to walk that direction, while others that you know may be called to go in a different direction. So it is a futile exercise to evaluate how well you are doing by comparing yourself with someone else.

Personal Notes

Personal Notes

Refuse to evaluate your life and ministry by any-thing except the Word of God and the calling that God has placed upon your life. That is the true test of being who you are really supposed to be and determining what you are to do with your life.

3. Believe in yourself and the ministry gift that God has given to you. If you don't believe in yourself, neither will anyone else. What you think of your-self is unconsciously projected to those around you, and they form similar opinions about you. As you raise your evaluation of yourself to what God has written in His Word about you, it will enable you to fulfill the ministry He has for you.

HEBREWS 10:35,36
Cast not away therefore your confidence, which hath great recompense of reward.
For ye have need of patience, that, after ye have done the will of God, ye might receive the promise.

God has placed great confidence in you! You must believe God's opinion of you so that you can rise up into His calling and ministry for your life. When you accept the opinion of mankind and fail to see yourself as God sees you, it robs you of the ability and motivation to walk in your God-given potential, not to mention all of the abundant blessings that are promised in His Word.

When you see that something in your life has not been developed to the point of being fruitful, or if you see that there is an area that isn't as it should be in your life or ministry, allow God to work in that area. Don't become discouraged or disheartened because you see things that need to be developed in your life and ministry. God will perfect what He has deposited in you as you follow His direction.

CONCLUSION

God expresses Himself in the earth through His Word, His Spirit, and His people. He has chosen you as a vessel to work through, and the more that you and God work together, the more you will allow God to flow through you in ministry. God will manifest Himself through you as you allow Him to use your personality and abilities for His glory.

In the process of perfecting your style, realize that God's input must happen so that His purposes and callings can be accomplished. God's efforts to perfect you are founded upon biblical principles. As you study the Scriptures, God will work those things into your life and ministry.

God will perfect you in your life and in your ministry! Today is the worst that you will ever be — tomorrow you will be better!

Personal Notes

2 TIMOTHY 3:16,17
All scripture is given by inspiration of God, and is profitable for doctrine, for reproof, for correction, for instruction in righteousness: That the man of God may be perfect, thoroughly furnished unto all good works.

28

Staying on Fire for God

One of the difficulties many ministers face is the ability to maintain their fire — their zeal and enthusiasm — for God and the ministry they have been called to fulfill. After several years of being in the ministry, many ministers simply go through the motions of doing their job.

So the challenge for ministers, including traveling ministers, is to continue being close to God, seeking God first above all else, and maintaining the same level of joy and excitement about the things of God. Notice what the prophet Jeremiah said about himself.

Personal Notes

JEREMIAH 20:9

Then I said, I will not make mention of him, nor speak any more in his name. But his word was in mine heart as a burning fire shut up in my bones, and I was weary with forbearing, and I could not stay.

The Apostle Paul used similar language in Philippians 3:8-14 to indicate his dedication, zeal, and fervor for God and the ministry.

PHILIPPIANS 3:8-14

Yea doubtless, and I count all things but loss for the excellency of the knowledge of Christ Jesus my Lord: for whom I have suffered the loss of all things, and do count them but dung, that I may win Christ,

And be found in him, not having mine own righteousness, which is of the law, but that which is through the faith of Christ, the righteousness which is of God by faith:

That I may know him, and the power of his resurrection, and the fellowship of his sufferings, being made conformable unto his death;

If by any means I might attain unto the resurrection of the dead.

Not as though I had already attained, either were already perfect: but I follow after, if that I may apprehend that for which also I am apprehended of Christ Jesus.

Brethren, I count not myself to have apprehended: but this one thing I do, forgetting those things which are behind, and reaching forth unto those things which are before,

I press toward the mark for the prize of the high calling of God in Christ Jesus.

The following material covers a list of issues that a minister must pay careful attention to so that he can finish his ministry with the same joy and fire he had when he started. A minister must not only start well, he must also finish well!

PERSONAL DEVOTION TIMES ARE A MUST

The Psalmist David knew the importance of maintaining a personal relationship with God and taking time to fellowship with God. It is easy to hear David's heart cry in this psalm as he verbalizes his dedication to God.

PSALM 5:1-3

Give ear to my words, O Lord, consider my meditation.

Hearken unto the voice of my cry, my King, and my God: for unto thee will I pray.

My voice shalt thou hear in the morning, O Lord; in the morning will I direct my prayer unto thee, and will look up.

Personal Notes

Personal Notes

A minister's priority and motivation as he seeks the face of God should be for his own well-being and because he loves God, not for the advancement of his ministry. Maintaining a personal relationship with God is a must in order to be an effective minister. No amount of knowledge or professional skills will take the place of your personal relationship with God. Resist the temptation to yield to the demands of the ministry that would make you substitute professional skills for your personal devotions in order to maintain your schedule.

However strange it may seem, it is true that as you guard your personal time with God, He will enhance your professional skills. Avoid resorting to mere methodology when ministering to the people. Methods are necessary, however they should never be a substitution for the revelation of the Word and the anointing that one receives as a result of spending time in the Presence of God.

Many ministers are confused and lack direction in their life because they have not developed a dynamic and living relationship with God. Times of fellowship where you commune with God are an absolute necessity in order to stay on track with God's plan for your life and ministry. In these times alone with the Father, you can consecrate yourself to the plan of God and allow God to take away any personal ambitions that may be within you.

Follow the example of Jesus in His earthly ministry. He never let anything or anyone disturb or distract Him from spending time with His Heavenly Father (Matthew 14:13, 23; 17:1; Mark 6:31,46; 9:2; Luke 6:12; 9:28). That was the key to the success of Jesus' ministry. He always knew what to say and what to do. Not once did Jesus have to say, "I just don't seem to have the answer today. Come back tomorrow." Because He spent personal time with His Heavenly Father, Jesus was prepared to minister whenever ministry was necessary. He didn't have to struggle to get the results that were needed for the people.

STUDY FOR YOURSELF, NOT FOR A MESSAGE

Here is the process of effectively communicating the Word of God. The revelation of God's Word must first speak to the minister before it can be spoken through the minister to others. A minister can only give to other people what God has given to him. So studying for yourself is an absolute necessity, for that is where God's approval is gained and real ministry is born.

2 TIMOTHY 2:15
Study to shew THYSELF approved unto God, a workman that needeth not to be ashamed, rightly dividing the word of truth.

Personal Notes

If the minister will study for his own edification and personal growth, he will become "the message" that is preached. The message that is in the Scriptures will be written upon his heart. The work that God does in a minister is often what the minister can communicate effectively to other people. Usually people must see the message working in the minister before they are willing to receive what he is saying.

Studying to get a sermon is work, and it drains the minister of his strength and wearies his flesh. Preparing a sermon is working for other people; it is not building up the minister. Putting a message together is part of the work of the ministry — it is not a part of a minister's relationship with God.

Studying for yourself is feeding your inner man, the human spirit, which gives you energy and strength. In order to continue effectively in ministry, you must learn to first minister to yourself. Then your heart and message will both be ready to minister to people.

MINISTER TO PEOPLE OUT OF YOUR OVERFLOW

As a minister you should learn to minister out of the abundance of your heart. Because you believe what you are saying, the message will be delivered with the spirit of faith that Paul referred to in Second Corinthians 4:13.

2 CORINTHIANS 4:13
We having the same spirit of faith, according as it is written, I believed, and therefore have I spoken; we also believe, and therefore speak.

Ministers should be overflowing with the things of God, speaking out of the abundance of the things of God within them. As a minister works on "filling up" personally on the things of God, a well-spring of revelation, power, and anointing will come out of him to minister to people.

A minister is the fountain through which the things of God should come flowing forth. Obviously if a minister does not spend any time with God personally, the things of God cannot come forth. A water fountain is connected to the source from which the water comes forth. In the same way, a minister must be connected with God so the things of God will come flowing forth.

This is how you will avoid "canned sermons" that have no life or power in them. Studying the Word, spending time in prayer, and seeking the face of God will bring life to a sermon, no matter how many times it is preached. The Word of God heard in the Presence of God as it is revealed to our hearts are words filled with life! When a minister speaks forth what he heard in the Presence of God, that same life that was conveyed to him will also be imparted to the people.

Personal Notes

ALLOW YOURSELF TO BE MOVED WITH COMPASSION

Compassion is the motivation of God — the reason why God ministers to people. Follow the example of Jesus as He was moved with compassion and ministered to the people around Him. Notice that whenever Jesus was moved with compassion, it motivated Him to take action to meet the needs of people.

MATTHEW 14:14
And Jesus went forth, and saw a great multitude, and WAS MOVED WITH COMPASSION TOWARD THEM, AND HE HEALED THEIR SICK.

(Also see Matthew 9:36; 15:32; 20:34; Mark 1:41; 5:19; 6:34; 8:2; 9:22; Luke 7:13.)

The Apostle Paul also stated that the love of God ruled over him, guiding his ministry to effectively minister to other people.

2 CORINTHIANS 5:14
For the love of Christ constraineth us; because we thus judge, that if one died for all, then were all dead.

Looking at the ministries of Jesus and the Apostle Paul reveals a pattern of effective ministry for ministers today. Compassion is a deep, inner yearning to do something that would help others. Compassion will rise up to minister to people as a minister looks at people the same way God sees them. People are valuable and precious — according to James 5:7, they are the precious fruit of the earth.

Refuse to know people after the flesh. Always allow the compassion and love of God to move you as you look at people. God loved people so much that He gave His Son Jesus Christ for their redemption. It was the highest price ever paid for anything. That is why people are the most valuable commodity in Heaven and on earth.

KEEP THE GIFT OF GOD STIRRED UP IN YOU

As you travel from church to church and continue the routine of meeting after meeting, sometimes you may wonder if you really have anything in you to minister to other people. You cannot go by your feelings or your emotions, because they are constantly subject to change. The devil would like for you to believe that you have no revelation of the Word of God to share and that you do not have the power of God available to minister to anyone.

However, you would do well to remember what the Apostle Paul told Timothy to do as a young minister.

Personal Notes

Personal Notes

_____

_____

_____

_____

_____

_____

_____

_____

_____

_____

_____

_____

_____

_____

_____

JOHN 6:63
It is the spirit that quick-
eneth; the flesh profiteth
nothing: the words that I
speak unto you, they are
spirit, and they are life.

2 TIMOTHY 1:6
Wherefore I put thee in remembrance that thou stir
up the gift of God, which is in thee by the putting on
of my hands.

Paul told Timothy to stir up the gift of God. You have to stir it up! Nobody can do it for you. First Samuel 30:6 says, "…David encouraged himself in the Lord his God." As a minister, periodically you have relive your calling, remember the times when God was faithful to you, and take time to count your blessings.

KEEPING PROPER PERSPECTIVE

Taking your eyes off of God and His ways and looking to man is a temptation that many ministers face. In keeping up with the demands of the ministry, at times you will get tired, and that is when you are most vulnerable to look at things from man's perspective instead of from God's viewpoint. God wants you to look at things the way that He does — that is why you have been given the written Word of God. As you study the Word of God you can learn God's thoughts and ways.

Has God ever told you to do something and then someone else comes along and informs you that it is not possible, or that even if it were possible, God would not use you to do it? Remember that ungodly counsel (something that contradicts the Word and callings of God) cannot help you fulfill what God has told you to do.

PSALM 1:1
Blessed is the man that walketh not in the counsel of the ungodly, nor standeth in the way of sinners, nor sitteth in the seat of the scornful.

Do not keep company with people who discourage you, criticize and magnify the faults of other people, or judge and condemn the Body of Christ. If you listen to people like that, every ember of the fire of God in you will die!

It is not wise to get your eyes on men. If you do, the faults, failures, and shortcomings of mankind will grow larger in your mind than the promises of God's Word. Continue to feast on the good Word of God. Spend time in the Presence of God until the world is washed out of your mind. Let God touch your life so profoundly until the love of God moves mightily within you. As you do these things, a raging fire from Heaven will begin to burn fiercely on the inside of you until it bursts forth and touches many people's lives!

Personal Notes

Personal Notes

CONCLUSION

The goal of ministers should be to speak words of life and be carriers of living water to people. Then people's lives will be changed by the power of God!

JOHN 6:63
It is the spirit that quickeneth; the flesh profiteth nothing: the words that I speak unto you, they are spirit, and they are life.

Jesus spoke words of life! He stayed focused upon His relationship with His Father. What He did in His earthly ministry was the result of knowing the Father, loving the Father, spending time with the Father, and obeying the Father.

This is a tremendous example for all ministers. If you want to stay on fire for God, you must do what Jesus did!

29

Your Image — How Others See You

In the Christian world dealing with your "image" is a often perceived as unscriptural, or certainly not Christ-like. When someone mentions the word "image," negative ideas of Hollywood and the values it promotes often come to many Christians' minds.

Let's define the word "image" to see what it really means. According to the dictionary, the word "image" means to portray or form a likeness of a person, or to mirror or reflect what a person really is. Therefore, "image" as used in this context is not portraying something that a person is not or displaying an exterior that is inconsistent

Personal Notes

with who a person really is. A Christian's image is to reflect as accurately as possible who they are in Christ.

From a practical viewpoint, your image consists of your attitude, actions, and appearance. All of these elements contribute to the total visible makeup of your image. The people around you can see all of these elements, and they form their opinion of you by what they see.

Your image will either hinder or help you in doing what God wants done. Some ministers have the things of God inside of them, but because their exterior doesn't reflect their interior, they are not successful. It is a proven fact that you must catch people's natural eye before they are willing to listen to the Word of God you want to share with them.

THE IMPORTANCE OF A GOOD ATTITUDE

Our attitude actually precedes us and gives people a preview of who we really are. People form their opinion of you by the attitudes you display. Remember what Zig Ziglar has often stated: "Sometimes we need a checkup from the neck up."

3 JOHN 1:2
Beloved, I wish above all things that thou mayest prosper and be in health, even as thy soul prospereth.

Notice that this verse states that you will experience prosperity and health according to the condition of your soul. In other words, your attitudes will greatly determine the success you experience.

Proverbs 23:7 says that as a man thinks in his heart, so is he. Some would argue that their attitude does not define who they really are. Some attitudes are temporary, nevertheless, they project an image of you at the time they are displayed.

Bad, negative, or hurtful attitudes will limit your success. Unforgiving, bitter, resentful, or critical attitudes will influence people to not have you in their church. Attitudes that are positive, confident, and good will help open doors of ministry to you. People are drawn to those who project the right kind of attitudes. Here are some attitudes that people are attracted to when they see them.

- **An enthusiastic attitude.** Enthusiasm is catching and will give people a desire to hook up with what you're doing.
- **An exciting attitude.** Excitement generates energy. Decide to be excited, and then you will feel excited. No one will become excited about what God is doing through you unless you first become excited.
- **A friendly, caring attitude.** Show that you care about other people. People don't care how much you know until they know how much you care.

Personal Notes

PROVERBS 18:24
A man that hath friends must show himself friendly: and there is a friend that sticketh closer than a brother.

Personal Notes

- **An attitude of appreciation.** Even a dog has enough sense to hang around where he is appreciated! By the same principle, people will also congregate where they are appreciated and valued. Cultivate an attitude of appreciation toward everyone who believes and participates in the will of God for your life.

- **An attitude of generosity.** People are attracted to givers. When the word spreads that you are a giver, pastors will seek you out to have you in their churches.

- **A considerate attitude.** Always be considerate and tolerant of others' feelings and values. Sometimes you can say things that are considerate but still not be considerate of others in the attitude you display.

- **A servant's attitude.** Always look for ways to help others. See what you can do to be a blessing to pastors when you speak at their churches. Your goal should be to have made a church better by the time you leave through your ministry to the people and your promotion of the pastor's vision while you were there.

Look at the way Daniel conducted himself in the palace. He had an excellent spirit within him and exhibited godly qualities. He knew how to properly present and conduct himself in the palace before the king. Because he had an excellent spirit within, Daniel did not neglect his outward image and appearance.

DANIEL 5:12

Forasmuch as an excellent spirit, and knowledge, and understanding, interpreting of dreams, and shewing of hard sentences, and dissolving of doubts, were found in the same Daniel, whom the king named Belteshazzar: now let Daniel be called, and he will show the interpretation.

DANIEL 6:3

Then this Daniel was preferred above the presidents and princes, because an excellent spirit was in him; and the king thought to set him over the whole realm.

As a traveling minister, you must not only have an excellent spirit within you (the proper attitudes), but you must also learn how to present yourself properly to a pastor, knowing how to conduct yourself in a confident, yet gentle manner. Pastors will often decide whether or not to have you in their church by what they see in your appearance and actions.

DEALING WITH YOUR APPEARANCE

Having the right appearance is just as important as having godly and moral qualities within you. You must upgrade both if you are going to be a successful minister.

Personal Notes

PROVERBS 17:27
He that hath knowledge spareth his words: and a man of understanding is of an excellent spirit.

Personal Notes

_____

_____

_____

_____

_____

_____

_____

_____

_____

_____

_____

_____

_____

_____

_____

_____

_____

Your appearance should reflect or compliment the qualities within you so that people will recognize your knowledge, qualities, gifts, and talents.

Your appearance will be a great factor in determining how you are received. Your appearance can open or close doors of opportunity for you to minister the Gospel of Jesus Christ. Always remember that people are moved by what they see.

> **1 SAMUEL 16:7 (NKJV)**
> **But the Lord said to Samuel, "Do not look at his appearance or at the height of his stature, because I have refused him. For the Lord does not see as man sees; for MAN LOOKS AT THE OUTWARD APPEARANCE, but the Lord looks at the heart."**

As ministers of God, we have a great treasure in us to share with other people — the Word of God. However, some people have hidden their treasure inside them in such a way that no one can see it, because they have not developed an image that is consistent with the treasure that is within them. Therefore they are limited in where they can go and in who will receive them.

Look at the example of Joseph. While Joseph was in prison, Pharaoh the king of Egypt requested that he tell Pharaoh's dream and the interpretation of it. It was Joseph's "big moment," and he immediately got ready for it.

GENESIS 41:14
Then Pharaoh sent and called Joseph, and they brought him hastily out of the dungeon: and he shaved himself, and changed his raiment, and came in unto Pharaoh.

It is interesting that Joseph took time to upgrade his appearance before he appeared in the palace. Not only did Joseph have the right words within him to share with Pharaoh, but he also looked, dressed, and conducted himself as if he had something to say. You must learn to resemble the message you share from the Word of God.

You may want to ask a close confidant about necessary changes that will help you improve your appearance. Make sure that the person you choose is experienced and qualified to give you the correct information you need. Select someone that will be honest but kind in his recommendations for change. His advice can be invaluable, especially if you are not knowledgeable of how to dress well, or you are not able to put colors together well.

Learn what hairstyles look good on you. Know the effect that facial hair such as beards, mustaches, etc. can have upon your appearance. Study books on dressing successfully and clothing catalogs until you can tell what

Personal Notes

Personal Notes

looks good on you and is appropriate for you as a minister of the Gospel.

Decide where you want to go and what you want to accomplish with your life. Then begin to study other people who are already successful in those same areas. What color suits, shoes, shirts, and accessories do they wear? What is the predominant hairstyle of the successful people in the vocation you are involved in? Do they have facial hair, or are they clean shaven?

Successful people know the value of proper appearance. One of the secrets of successful people is that their hairstyle and clothing reflect what they are attempting to accomplish. It can help them get the job done.

Appearance can cause people to either raise or lower their expectations of you. Endeavor to develop your appearance in such a way that it helps other people receive the Gospel. There should not be any discrepancy between your appearance and the message you preach. Continue to upgrade your appearance until it compliments the the Gospel of Jesus Christ that you preach.

CONDUCTING YOURSELF PROPERLY

Actions speak louder than words. Your actions convey a message to other people about what kind of person you are. People watch how you respond to certain situations and draw their conclusions about you from what they see. If you want to see what a person is really like, watch him at a time when he is under pressure.

Whatever is on the inside of him will show itself at that time.

Learning protocol, manners, and proper etiquette is necessary so that you can conduct yourself properly in the ministry. Proper etiquette is needed, whether you are meeting a pastor for coffee, visiting in someone's home, or preaching a message at a church.

Conducting yourself in the right way will help other people receive you as a minister of the Gospel and make them more willing to hear you minister the Gospel of Jesus Christ. Our goal should be to reach as many people for Christ as we can. Therefore everything should be geared toward this end — that people would receive you, the way you conduct yourself, and ultimately receive the message of Jesus Christ.

UPGRADING TO A NEW LEVEL

At one time in the traveling ministry, I asked a pastor friend what I could do to bring increase to my traveling ministry. His comment to me was, "I think you have an image problem." Although that comment didn't exactly make my day, it became the catalyst that caused me to improve my image, and as a result I began to experience increase in my traveling ministry.

If you want to move up to another level in the traveling ministry, you must consider upgrading your image. Sir Francis Bacon said, "He that will not apply new remedies

Personal Notes

must expect new evils." If you do not change your image, people will not expect or receive anything new from you. If this is continues to happen, your traveling ministry will actually regress, rather than increase.

People will always look at the visible part of you to see if anything about you has changed. People have to see something different about you before they can recognize that you are not what you used to be. Remember that God said in First Samuel 16:7, "But the Lord said unto Samuel, Look not on his countenance, or on the height of his stature; because I have refused him: for the Lord seeth not as man seeth; for man looketh on the outward appearance, but the Lord looketh on the heart."

There are various things to consider when upgrading your appearance. Here is a list of things that a traveling minister needs to consider and make changes accordingly.

- Your spiritual condition — that alone will change your countenance
- Your clothes (the way you dress)
- Your hairstyle
- Your manners
- Your communication skills
- Your literature (brochures, business cards, etc.)
- Your tapes and books
- Your presentation of God's Word
- Your revelation and anointing by which you minister

CONCLUSION

As a traveling minister, you must have the anointing of God on you and the Word of God in you to be effective. You should make every effort to have both of these things. However, paying attention to your image will also help you be successful in ministry.

People can recognize the spiritual change that has occurred in you as you pay attention to your image and make the changes that are necessary. Listen to the Spirit of God, and He will guide you in your natural appearance as well as in spiritual things.

Be encouraged by the Psalmist's words: "I will instruct you (says the Lord) and guide you along the best pathway of life; I will advise you and watch your progress" (Ps. 32:8 TLB). God will help you look your best!

Personal Notes

Preaching Effectively

Communicating With Relevance

Considering Your Audience

Cultural Issues in Ministry

30

Communicating With Relevance

The challenge for ministers today is to be as relevant as possible with an unchanging message to an audience who is constantly evaluating and changing their needs, desires, perspectives, values, and beliefs. Getting people to relate, trust, and commit to something that is several millenniums old is the task of the modern day preacher.

This task of being relevant is multiplied times more difficult for the traveling minister as he ministers in different cities and communities. He has to learn how to relate, not only to one audience, but to many different groups of people with all kinds of backgrounds, values, beliefs, and cultures.

Several years ago I ministered in a multi-ethnic church in the heart of a major city, and two days later I ministered in a predominantly-white church located in a rural area. I could not minister to the inner-city congregation the same way I did to the audience in the country. I preached the same message, but my approach had to be different in order to reach the different audiences.

The word "relevance" as defined in the Scribner-Bantam Dictionary gives the idea of relating to the case at hand, being pertinent, adapted, appropriate, congruent, or agreeable. In order to communicate with relevance, we must preach the unchangeable Gospel message in an pertinent, adapted, appropriate, congruent, or agreeable way.

Why is relevance needed? So the people will see that the Word of God contains answers relevant to their situation and needs and thus open their hearts to receive what they need from the Word of God.

Preachers, and Christians in general, are often accused of being archaic and out of touch and of adhering to a set of medieval ideas that have no meaning in our modern society. Some ministers do need to change their style, methods, and ways of communicating in an effort to relate more effectively to an audience. What may have worked fifty years ago may not be the best way to relate to the present generation.

BIBLICAL EXAMPLES OF RELEVANCE

There are numerous examples in the Scriptures where Jesus and the apostles made great effort to be relevant to their audience when communicating the truth of God's Word. In His earthly ministry, Jesus made every attempt possible to present the Gospel in a way that related to the audience. One of the most striking examples of relevance occurred when Jesus ministered to the woman at the well outside a village in Samaria. What Jesus said to the woman related to her needs and was pertinent to the problems and surroundings at hand.

JOHN 4:5-26 (NKJV)
So He came to a city of Samaria which is called Sychar, near the plot of ground that Jacob gave to his son Joseph.
Now Jacob's well was there. Jesus therefore, being wearied from His journey, sat thus by the well. It was about the sixth hour.
A woman of Samaria came to draw water. Jesus said to her, "Give Me a drink."
For His disciples had gone away into the city to buy food.
Then the woman of Samaria said to Him, "How is it that You, being a Jew, ask a drink from me, a Samaritan woman?" For Jews have no dealings with Samaritans.

Jesus answered and said to her, "If you knew the gift of God, and who it is who says to you, 'Give Me a drink,' you would have asked Him, and He would have given you living water."

The woman said to Him, "Sir, You have nothing to draw with, and the well is deep. Where then do You get that living water?

"Are You greater than our father Jacob, who gave us the well, and drank from it himself, as well as his sons and his livestock?"

Jesus answered and said to her, "Whoever drinks of this water will thirst again,

"but whoever drinks of the water that I shall give him will never thirst. But the water that I shall give him will become in him a fountain of water springing up into everlasting life."

The woman said to Him, "Sir, give me this water, that I may not thirst, nor come here to draw."

Jesus said to her, "Go, call your husband, and come here."

The woman answered and said, "I have no husband." Jesus said to her, "You have well said, 'I have no husband,'

"for you have had five husbands, and the one whom you now have is not your husband; in that you spoke truly."

The woman said to Him, "Sir, I perceive that You are a prophet.

"Our fathers worshiped on this mountain, and you Jews say that in Jerusalem is the place where one ought to worship."

Jesus said to her, "Woman, believe Me, the hour is coming when you will neither on this mountain, nor in Jerusalem, worship the Father.

"You worship what you do not know; we know what we worship, for salvation is of the Jews.

"But the hour is coming, and now is, when the true worshipers will worship the Father in spirit and truth; for the Father is seeking such to worship Him.

"God is Spirit, and those who worship Him must worship in spirit and truth."

The woman said to Him, "I know that Messiah is coming" (who is called Christ). "When He comes, He will tell us all things."

Jesus said to her, "I who speak to you am He."

Notice how Jesus referred to the well, the water, the woman's marital status, and the mountain nearby. Jesus did all of that so the woman could relate to the spiritual message He shared with her and become willing to receive the truth into her life.

We have another example of preaching the Gospel with relevance in the Apostle Paul's preaching on Mars' Hill in Athens. It is interesting to note how Paul took time to notice the condition of the people, how they thought, their customs, and what their needs were before he spoke to them.

Personal Notes

Personal Notes

_____

_____

_____

_____

_____

_____

_____

_____

_____

_____

_____

_____

_____

_____

_____

_____

_____

_____

_____

_____

_____

_____

ACTS 17:22-34 (NKJV)

Then Paul stood in the midst of the Areopagus and said, "Men of Athens, I perceive that in all things you are very religious;

"for as I was passing through and considering the objects of your worship, I even found an altar with this inscription: TO THE UNKNOWN GOD. Therefore, the One whom you worship without knowing, Him I proclaim to you:

"God, who made the world and everything in it, since He is Lord of heaven and earth, does not dwell in temples made with hands.

"Nor is He worshiped with men's hands, as though He needed anything, since He gives to all life, breath, and all things.

"And He has made from one blood every nation of men to dwell on all the face of the earth, and has determined their preappointed times and the boundaries of their habitation,

"so that they should seek the Lord, in the hope that they might grope for Him and find Him, though He is not far from each one of us;

"for in Him we live and move and have our being, as also some of your own poets have said, 'For we are also His offspring.'

"Therefore, since we are the offspring of God, we ought not to think that the Divine Nature is like gold or silver or stone, something shaped by art and man's devising.

"Truly, these times of ignorance God overlooked, but now commands all men everywhere to repent,

"because He has appointed a day on which He will judge the world in righteousness by the Man whom He has ordained. He has given assurance of this to all by raising Him from the dead."
And when they heard of the resurrection of the dead, some mocked, while others said, "We will hear you again on this matter."
So Paul departed from among them.
However, some men joined him and believed, among them Dionysius the Areopagite, a woman named Damaris, and others with them.

Paul began his message by addressing the nature of the people there (very religious), calling their attention to something familiar to them (the statue to the unknown god), and then relating the true God as the unknown god who is now making Himself known to them. Paul finished by giving the people instructions to repent and turn to the living God. As a result, some scoffed at him, but a number of people responded to the message and believed.

The Apostle Paul stated his philosophy of ministry in 1 Corinthians 9:19-23. This passage explains that Paul's methods and styles of ministry were an effort to reach every person that he could with the Gospel of Jesus Christ. He was willing to adapt his presentation to the audience so that they would be willing to listen to the Gospel.

Personal Notes

Personal Notes

I CORINTHIANS 9:19-23 (NKJV)

For though I am free from all men, I have made myself a servant to all, that I might win the more;

and to the Jews I became as a Jew, that I might win Jews; to those who are under the law, as under the law, that I might win those who are under the law;

to those who are without law, as without law (not being without law toward God, but under law toward Christ), that I might win those who are without law;

to the weak I became as weak, that I might win the weak. I have become all things to all men, that I might by all means save some.

Now this I do for the gospel's sake, that I may be partaker of it with you.

UNDERSTANDING HUMAN NATURE

One of the most important things a minister can do other than study the Bible and know God, is to study human nature. Ministers are in the people business, and they should know how people function to some degree. Knowing human nature is vital to a minister's success and effectiveness, just as knowing how a car functions is a vital part of a mechanic's success.

A minister must learn the answers to questions such as:

- What are the basic needs of humanity?
- What motivates a group of people?

- What is the current situation and surroundings of particular people groups?
- How do people digest and process new information until it is incorporated into their lifestyle?
- What are the biggest concerns and fears that the people have?
- What principles will lead people to make a decision that is necessary to reach a desired conclusion?

In his book <u>Keys to Better Preaching</u>, John Garlock shares about the necessity of having insight into human nature: "…a preacher cannot reject the facts of human psychology. People think in certain ways, and are led to conclusions according to identifiable principles. Jesus employed excellent psychology when He said, 'he that is without sin among you, let him cast the first stone' (John 8:7). Paul had keen psychological insight when he shouted to a crowd that was half Pharisee and half Sadducee, '…I am a Pharisee, the son of a Pharisee…'(Acts 23:6)."

CONNECTING WITH PEOPLE

One of the phrases that you currently hear as people talk about relating properly with one another is "connecting with people." This simply refers to someone who makes an effort to communicate in such a way that it relates to people and thereby effectively touches their lives.

Personal Notes

As a minister, you must somehow touch people's hearts before asking them to make commitment to the Gospel. When you attempt to understand people, it sends a message to them that you are their friend. By simply being warm, approachable, and caring, people will much more readily receive what you have to say.

In his book The 21 Irrefutable Laws of Leadership, John Maxwell states, "All great communicators recognize this truth [connecting with people] and act on it instinctively. You can't move people to action unless you first move them with emotion. The heart comes before the head."

Always remember that even in a large crowd, you are still speaking to individuals. Don't just speak to the crowd in general; instead, speak specifically to people's needs. See their individuality and that God has created each of them personally.

General Norman Schwarzkopf remarked, "I have seen competent leaders who stood in front of a platoon and all they saw was a platoon. But great leaders stand in front of a platoon and see it as forty-four individuals, each of whom has aspirations, each of whom wants to live, each of whom wants to do good."

Remember when attempting to be relevant that people are individuals, and they all have a heart to believe, emotions to feel, and a mind to process and store the truths that you share. If you will connect with their heart and emotions, often you can get them to make a decision in their mind to respond to the truth of God's Word.

COMMON INTEREST THEMES

Did you ever notice that commercials on television are designed to be relevant to the typical person watching the program in which they appear. Marketing experts carefully match commercials with programs that have a common interest theme. They are maximizing the results of their marketing program by buying advertising time on programs that people who would be interested in buying their products are probably already watching.

One aspect of being relevant with the message of the Gospel is to identify and communicate the common interests that the audience may have. As a minister learns to do this, the audience will sense that the minister understands and cares about their situation, and thus become open to hear the solutions that the minister shares from the Word of God.

Jesus did this by referring to what was at hand — water, stones, mountains, trees, the social and religious cultures and beliefs, and the needs and desires of people. Often He would use a parable — an earthly story that had a spiritual meaning or truth — to convey the truths that He wanted the people to hear.

Personal Notes

An effective minister must seek to find common ground with people before sharing a spiritual truth as the answer to their problems. When ministering to a particular audience learn to ask yourself questions such as the following.

- What are the people's interests, hobbies, desires, and dreams?
- If you were in the other person's shoes, how would you respond to the truth of God's Word?
- What common problems have you and the people experienced?

As you take the time to become observant of people's conditions, surroundings, and situations, you will be able to identify themes that people can relate to and then respond to the truth of God's Word as the answer.

TOUCHING THE EMOTIONS

As a minister who relates the spiritual truths of the Scriptures, you must remember that people must process those truths within them before they accept and incorporate those spiritual truths into their lifestyles. Often it takes time for an individual to be willing to incorporate truth into his life.

If a minister merely communicates information or facts that can be processed intellectually, he will be unable to move people beyond their current situation or condition in any significant manner or degree. While a minister must have significant content and information in his message, having these alone falls far short of what a minister's task is really all about. Ministers are not called to simply convey information — they are called to be vessels through which the truths of God's Word are communicated in such a way that it relates to people intellectually, emotionally, and spiritually.

It is a fact well worth observing that people generally do not respond to something unless it touches their emotions. There are a few people who are spiritual enough to disregard their emotions when receiving spiritual truths, but the majority of people you will minister to will process truth through their emotions. If this is true, instead of becoming frustrated at the "obvious carnality of the people," it may be wise to communicate to people in such a way that both the heart and the emotions are touched.

THE ANOINTING AND POWER OF GOD

Here is a question that the ministers of today must come to terms with: Does a minister have to utilize the electronic media in an effort to stay relevant with people today?

In our society, we are living in an electronic age where data and information is processed at a very rapid pace. People are inundated from every direction with facts and figures, and new technology is being developed at an amazingly fast rate. It may be tempting for some ministers to get caught up in using all of the latest technology in an effort to relate to the people they are ministering to.

The current generation, especially teenagers and young people, have grown up in this high-tech way of life. Their values and ways of thinking have been greatly influenced by all of the electronic technology available today. If a minister is ministering to youth or children, using electronic technology may help get their attention and hold their interest — but you must still present the truths of God's Word with the anointing and power of God.

Electronic media can help people to receive the Gospel message, but it should not be a substitute for the anointing and power of God. The Holy Spirit can accomplish in a moment what no man can do in a lifetime with all the electronic technology in the world.

JOHN 16:7-11,13 (NKJV)
"Nevertheless I [Jesus] tell you the truth. It is to your advantage that I go away; for if I do not go away, the Helper will not come to you; but if I depart, I will send Him to you.
"And when He has come, He will convict the world of sin, and of righteousness, and of judgment:
"of sin, because they do not believe in Me;
"of righteousness, because I go to My Father and you see Me no more;
"of judgment, because the ruler of this world is judged....

"However, when He, the Spirit of truth, has come, He will guide you into all truth; for He will not speak on His own authority, but whatever He hears He will speak; and He will tell you things to come."

The Holy Spirit has the ability to penetrate the hearts and minds of people with the relevance of the Gospel. He can reach into the deep recesses of a person's heart and convict him of the need for the truth of God's Word. He makes the Word come alive to an individual until the Gospel seems to be the most relevant and pertinent answer that he has ever heard.

CONCLUSION

Thank God for the great strides that have been made in ministry by utilizing technology, understanding human nature, connecting with people, and developing common interest themes. However, we must always remember that along with all of those things, we must still depend upon the Holy Spirit to help us reach people with the Gospel of Jesus Christ. He can do what no one else can!

Personal Notes

31

Considering Your Audience

As we learned in the previous lesson, the way you relate to your audience will greatly effect your effectiveness as a minister. In this lesson, we are going to look at some elements to consider as you put your sermon together. Some questions that will be answered include:

- What is needed to reach the people who are going to be listening to you?
- What is the response that you desire to see in the people?
- How can you present your message to get the desired response from your audience?

Some of the material in this lesson has been adapted from <u>The Spoken Word</u> by William N. Brigance, which was published in 1906. The principles of reaching your audience that Brigance shares in his book are still applicable today.

According to Brigance, there are two primary issues that a minister must address as he preaches if he wants to see visible results in the audience. The first issue is to gain the interest of the audience, and the second issue is to attempt to persuade the people to respond to the message.

CREATING INTEREST IN YOUR AUDIENCE

If you can gain the interest of your audience, you have their attention. Interest and attention work together. In order to sustain the interest and attention of your audience you must keep the line of thought moving. Avoid getting "bogged down" with a thought and dwelling upon it too long.

Today's audience is a TV generation and is used to sound and movement. If you want to hold their interest, you must move along with the thoughts you present. Learn to present your thoughts in "bite-sized" pieces of information.

Every minister should realize that he needs a "tool chest" where he keeps various tools that help him sustain the interest and attention of the audience. Some of these tools include:

1. **Bible Principles** — This refers to Biblical truths that are presented factually and pictorially in such a way that it makes an impact upon people's lives. Always remember that the truths of the Bible contain the power of God to set people free.

2. **Suspense** — This is where you present your message in such a way that people are unable to forecast the outcome. Using this tool requires a great deal of skill in holding people's interest and yet not revealing the outcome until the right moment.

3. **Activities** — Using activities such as drama, skits, demonstrations, visuals, etc. help keep the interest level high. Two words of advice concerning visuals: (1) make them so the people can understand them quickly and read them easily, and (2) show your visuals in short segments of time to break up your session. Remember that many people are used to a commercial break every ten minutes because they watch television.

4. **Antagonism** — This consists of telling stories of conflict, or making conflicting or controversial statements. Wield this tool very carefully so that you do not inflict damage on other people. You do not want to use this tool so much that you become known as an antagonistic minister.

Personal Notes

However, as a tool that is used in a limited way, it can be very effective to get people's attention.

5. **Humor** — Humor is one of the most effective tools you can use, but it is also hard to use well. Most people who use humor overuse it until they either look like clowns or the people have forgotten the spiritual truths that were trying to be communicated to them. Several words of advice: (1) avoid the "clownish" level, (2) use jokes carefully, and (3) be accurate in your quotes, stories, comparisons, exaggeration, etc.

6. **The Familiar** — Beginning your message with a truth, principle, or incident that people are familiar with before presenting something new is an effective way to gain the confidence, trust, and willingness of the people to receive what you have to say. One principle of learning is that when a new truth is taught, it must be based upon truth that the people already know.

7. **Human Interest Topics or Stories** — This tool is a great way to identify with the people and to show that you understand what they are dealing with.

THE ART OF PERSUASION

The fine art of persuasion is not to be confused with manipulation. Persuading someone to respond to the Gospel means that you allow them to make a free will choice. Manipulation pressures a person to do something against his will, even if it is not to his benefit to do so.

It is important that you make some attempt to understand human nature if you want to persuade people to acknowledge, accept, and embrace the truths that you are presenting to them. Persuading people includes the process of getting their undivided attention and influencing their will.

Look at the example of Abraham. He listened and pondered the things that God had told him until he was fully persuaded that God would do what He had promised. Romans 4:21 tells us that Abraham was "fully persuaded that, what he had promised, he [God] was able also to perform."

Because Abraham became fully persuaded, or convinced, that God would do what He had promised, Abraham received what had been promised. If you study Abraham's walk with God, you will find that God spoke to Abraham several times over a period of years. This shows that it is a process for a person to become fully persuaded about something.

The Apostle Paul was brought before King Agrippa because he was accused by the Jews. The Apostle Paul took the opportunity to give a stirring account of how God had worked in his life. Everything he said was an attempt to persuade King Agrippa to believe in Jesus Christ as his Saviour. Finally Paul asked King Agrippa a question: "King Agrippa, believest thou the prophets?..." (Acts 26:27).

Personal Notes

Now notice King Agrippa's response: " . . . Almost thou persuadest me to be a Christian" (Acts 26:28).

We see in this scripture that King Agrippa was almost persuaded to become a Christian. The Apostle Paul had set a goal to do all he could to convince King Agrippa to become a Christian, and King Agrippa was almost convinced to do so.

As we examine the nature of persuasion, there is no one thing that will cause people to become convinced of what a minister presents to them. Various elements will come to play in the different settings that the traveling minister is in. However, in examining the persuasion process in many different ministry settings, all of these elements can be categorized into four major factors.

The first factor is the work of the Holy Spirit. Never underestimate the power of the Holy Spirit to penetrate the heart of a person to convince them of the validity and relevance of the Word of God. The Holy Spirit has no limitations of time or distance, and He can deal with a person no matter where they are, even when they are all alone.

JOHN 16:7-8 (NKJV)
"Nevertheless I [Jesus] tell you the truth. It is to your advantage that I go away; for if I do not go away, the Helper will not come to you; but if I depart, I will send Him to you.
"And when He has come, He will convict the world of sin, and of righteousness, and of judgment."

1 CORINTHIANS 2:9-13 (NKJV)
But as it is written: "Eye has not seen, nor ear heard, nor have entered into the heart of man the things which God has prepared for those who love Him." But God has revealed them to us through His Spirit. For the Spirit searches all things, yes, the deep things of God. For what man knows the things of a man except the spirit of the man which is in him? Even so no one knows the things of God except the Spirit of God. Now we have received, not the spirit of the world, but the Spirit who is from God, that we might know the things that have been freely given to us by God.

The effective minister must learn to cooperate with the Holy Spirit and work in a partnership together to persuade the listener of the Truth. The minister cannot do the job alone, and the Holy Spirit is looking for willing vessels to work through. Although the Holy Spirit is sovereign is His decisions and distributions of gifts, He works sovereignly through willing and cooperating ministers to accomplish the will of God in the lives of people.

So the first and greatest factor in the persuasion process is the work of the Holy Spirit. Every minister must be in communication with the Holy Spirit to effectively persuade people to respond to the Gospel of Jesus Christ.

The second factor to consider is the subject. First, the subject must be biblical if we are going to obtain godly results. Social discourses, civil rights speeches, political

Personal Notes

rhetoric, and documentaries all have their place. But the minister of God is called to share Biblical truths because that is what sets people free.

JOHN 8:31,32 (NKJV)
Then Jesus said to those Jews who believed Him, "If you abide in My word, you are My disciples indeed. "And you shall know the truth, and the truth shall make you free."

How you handle your subject will greatly determine what the Holy Spirit can do and whether or not the people will accept what is said as the truth. Aim precisely at what you want to accomplish. Make sure that your subject is properly organized so that the people can follow you step-by-step toward the projected goal. Present your facts accurately and use illustrations when necessary so that the people can understand clearly what God wants them to do. Some of the most successful ministers are able to paint word pictures in the minds of the listeners so that the people can easily see where to go.

Use your subject to reach out and touch people and convince them of the wonderful promises of God's Word. Avoid getting so caught up in your subject that you forget to convince the people of the goodness of God. Your subject is not an end in itself; it is a means to persuade people to follow God and walk in His blessings.

The speaker is the third factor in the persuasion process. The character, attitude, and personality of the minister will help greatly in creating favorable feelings in your audience. Having bad attitudes, immoral character, or a grating personality can arouse feelings of hostility toward you, which will affect how the people receive the truth of God's Word.

Issues such as strong moral character, self-control, discipline, sincerity, and earnestness can help a minister be credible in the eyes of the people. People will also open their heart more readily when a warm, caring attitude is displayed. Let the truth of God's Word penetrate your own heart before you attempt to persuade others with it. In other words, the old saying is still true: "Practice what you preach."

Always remember to be respectful, courteous, and fair with people. We must treat people with decent kindness. Even in times when disagreements or conflicts occur, we must always strive to be as tactful as possible with our words. Proverbs 16:21 reveals that "...sweetness of the lips increases learning" (NKJV). It may take some thought to present the truth of God's Word in such a way that it deals with the issues and does not offend people.

The fourth and last factor to consider is the audience itself. Often people are simply waiting to hear what you have to say before they anticipate receiving anything from

Personal Notes

God. By not anticipating to receive anything, they have assumed the role of passive opposition. They are waiting for you to convince them. People may even want to be convinced, but they are waiting for you to persuade them. So the challenge that lies in front of every minister is to take the people from passivity to being fully persuaded of the truth of God's Word!

There are various ways a minister can overcome an audience's passive opposition. You can use how-to suggestions, giving successful examples and clear explanations. Addressing social pressures such as following the crowd, the desire for approval, trying to live up to others' expectations, peer pressure, and rivalry can be used as an appeal to bring about behavioral change.

At times a minister may find himself in a situation where the people actively oppose him or what he has said. So a minister may have to get himself out of a tough situation even if the situation was no fault of his own. There are several things that a minister can do to help defuse such a situation.

Make every effort to avoid arguments, because they are often ineffective and tend to arouse opposition. People tend to get emotional in arguments and may respond illogically even to the best of arguments. Mental stereotypes and preconceived ideas may impel people to accept or reject arguments regardless of their soundness.

You may want to humbly express an apology for what happened, even if it was not your fault. This will help set the atmosphere for further repentance and correction. When people see the minister set a godly example, it is often the catalyst for them to respond in a godly manner.

Also recognize and minister to the basic emotional needs that people have, such as love, acceptance, recognition, appreciation, fulfillment, purpose, etc. This can help overcome strife, prejudices, preconceived ideas, and hatred that may have existed within the people.

Every person was created with basic needs and desires, and they need to be assured of them. People are created in such a way that they need security and protection, the ability to acquire provision, social standing, emotional wholeness, assurance of spiritual well-being, etc. As you minister the Word of God, begin to assure them that God and you are for them and want them to experience all that God created them to have.

Being in a situation where you are being actively opposed is not a very good experience. However, with the wisdom of God, and knowing certain things about human nature, it is possible to come out of those situations successfully.

Personal Notes

Personal Notes

CONCLUSION

Considering your audience is essential if you are going to minister successfully. You are in the people business, and the reason you are a minister is to help people successfully negotiate the process of change and receive all that God has for them.

32

Cultural Issues In Ministry

As a traveling minister, you will be required to minister in various areas across the United States and deal with various cultures. You will quickly find that people in different areas respond in different ways. A minister must learn how to deal with culture as he presents an unchanging God with a timeless message of redemption and blessing. George Barna stated, "God hasn't changed in over 1,000,000 years, but our culture is redefined every 3-5 years."

Observing culture will give a person insight into the way people think and how a person can relate to an audience culturally in order to preach the Gospel effectively. Inroads can be made into the hearts of people when you understand their culture and adapt your message of truth so they can relate to it.

DEFINING CULTURE

Culture refers to the way of life of a group of people. In his book Survival Kit for Overseas Living, L. Robert Kohls states, "Culture is an integrated system of learned behavior patterns that are characteristic of any given society. Culture refers to the total way of life of particular groups of people. It includes everything that a group of people thinks, says, does, and makes — its system of attitudes and feelings. Culture is learned and transmitted from generation to generation."

Culture is formed by the rules that people live by. For example, the Christian culture is formed by the commandments of the Bible, especially Jesus' commandment of love found in John 13:34,35.

Culture is formed by the needs of the people, such as their basic need for food, shelter, and clothing. As people's needs change, so will their culture.

Culture is formed by the beliefs that people embrace. People's beliefs can change, and this will affect their culture. For example, when a person accepts Christ as his Savior, his beliefs and convictions changed. This causes him to change his way of life.

Culture is formed by the values people integrate into their lifestyles. A Christian's values are quite different than those of unbelievers. People who were born in the Far East were taught a different value system than those who grew up in a Western culture.

Culture is formed by people's perspective of things. A person's perspective is determined by his position in relation to a certain thing or issue. The Apostle Paul's views changed with his conversion. When Paul changed his position from a sinner to a born-again person, his perspective changed concerning God and the way that a child of God was supposed to act.

Culture can be formed by the teachings that people receive from their parents, school, and church. Culture can be formed by anything that people allow to have input into the way they live their lives.

AMERICA — A LAND OF MANY CULTURES

America has been called the "melting pot of the world." In other words, America is a land of diversity. Many different nationalities are represented in America, and as a result, many different cultures can be found. In America, there are people from every continent in the world. There are people of European, African, Spanish, Latin, Russian, Asian, and Indian descent — just to name a few! All these people of different nationalities live

Personal Notes

in one country along with the Native Americans who were on the land before anyone else.

Not only is America a land with people from many different nations, but its vast acreage includes many different geographical and climatic areas. The geographical areas includes swamp, dry desert area, mountains, rich farm ground, vast grassy plains, sea coasts, lakes and rivers, and forests filled with beautiful and gigantic trees. The climate ranges from places having six months of cold winter every year to places where it is always summertime. In some places it is very dry, and in other places the rainfall is abundant.

The various population levels in cities, towns, and villages also create various cultures throughout America. People who grew up in a rural area think, act, and respond differently than people who live in a large metropolitan area. Those who grew up in the inner-city ghettos have a different perspective of life than those who grew up in affluent areas.

Other influences upon the American people include various religious beliefs, educational philosophies, technological advances, and social changes. Because these influences are constantly developing, evolving, and growing, the American culture is constantly changing. According to Stephanie Edwards, a marketing consultant, because of the heavy influence of television today, American culture is a culture of "see and want" rather than "think and do." Our American culture is characterized by the following:

1. A culture of convenience — a soft, easy lifestyle, where everything is easily obtained, and a prevailing attitude that "the world owes me...."

2. A culture of compromise — the philosophy of relativism, situational ethics, and no absolutes coupled with rejecting the relevancy of the Bible today.

3. A culture of courage — the "home of the free and the land of the brave." Today our courage has gone awry, being detached from any moral and spiritual values and now shows itself as anarchy and rebellion.

4. A culture of change — the constant shift change is one of the biggest stress factors in America today.

5. A culture of no convictions — no deep-seated beliefs or willingness to take a stand on issues.

6. A culture of competition — a world of financial pressure, cut-throat business practices with no conscience, and aggressive guerilla marketing is ingrained in the American mind.

7. A culture of confusion and chaos — because of the myriad of laws enacted by our government

Personal Notes

every year and the conflicting values seen from one culture to the next.

8. A culture of creativity — the freedom of expression guaranteed by our Constitution has produced an atmosphere of unprecedented creativity and exploration.

Another factor in American culture is the different generations that currently exist. There are the "baby builders" who were born prior to 1946; the "baby boomers" who were born between 1946 and 1964; and the "baby busters," including those who were born between 1965 and 1983. Since then, Generation X and others have come into existence. Each generation will relate differently to the Gospel of Jesus Christ because of the different time periods in which they grew up and the changing world around them.

THE CHRISTIAN CULTURE

Christianity has never been understood by the world, because they have not understood the foundation on which it was founded — the Cross of Jesus Christ. The ideals, beliefs, and values within the Church world, or Christian culture, are vastly different than those of the world — as far apart as one planet is from another.

As you travel to different churches, the congregations will be different because of the culture in which they live and because of where the church is located. People do not leave their culture outside when they come into the church building to worship God. For this reason, churches in the city are vastly different from churches in the country.

An interesting observation is how small churches (less than one hundred members) often have a different philosophy of ministry and conduct their services differently than a larger church. Small churches are more concerned with relationships, family and relatives, simplicity, traditions, and stability. While larger churches are also concerned about relationships, family, and stability, they approach these issues differently than small churches do. Utilizing talents in the congregation, being vision oriented, staying on schedule, using electronic technology, and selecting the right staff are other issues facing a larger church.

In the midst of the diversity that can be found in the Christian community, a traveling minister must be willing to adapt but not compromise his beliefs. Be firmly established in your beliefs, and at the same time, embrace the diversity of culture found within the church world.

Make every effort to speak the same "language." In other words, find some common ground that both you and the people are familiar with and can agree on. In Leadership magazine, Calvin Thomsen commented, "I don't say anything I don't believe, but I am careful to say things in the way people need to hear it." This reflects an

Personal Notes

effort to present a message of God's Word in such a way that people will understand and receive it.

Be able to laugh at yourself, enjoying the differences that exist between you and other people. The church rests upon the foundation of Christ, not upon your abilities, ideas, or correct doctrine. So don't take yourself too seriously. Be willing to admit that you do not know it all. Laugh at your mistakes, especially when they occur in public. People like being around someone who can laugh at himself.

SCRIPTURALLY DEALING WITH CULTURE

Someone may legitimately ask, "Doesn't the Word of God take precedence over culture and customs? Why not just preach the Word in principle, and let God deal with the people?"

In every case, the Word of God must take precedence over culture and customs in order for the people to benefit from it. People must become convinced that according to the Scriptures salvation is by faith in Jesus Christ and His redemptive work at the Cross. Otherwise they are not in a position to believe the Scriptures, and thus cannot receive Christ as their Savior.

Yet the wise minister will seek to find common or familiar ground with the people before he begins to expound upon the Scriptures and the fact that Christ is the only way unto salvation. Once a minister indicates that he respects likes the people and their culture, the people are much more apt to receive the message of Christ. In <u>Leadership</u> magazine, Susan Baker made this comment: "It isn't important that the minister be like the people. What is important is that he likes the people and that they know it."

In his book <u>Survival Kit for Overseas Living</u>, L. Robert Kohls answers the question as to why culture must be dealt with in ministry. Kohls said that "...every group of people, every culture, is, and has always been ethnocentric; that is, it thinks its own solutions are superior and would be recognized as superior by any right-thinking, intelligent, logical human being." Of course the Scriptures also indicate that a person's way of life, thinking, and conduct is usually justified in his or her own mind, even if it leads him or her into destruction and death.

PROVERBS 16:2,25 (NKJV)
All the ways of a man are pure in his own eyes, But the Lord weighs the spirits....
There is a way that seems right to a man, But its end is the way of death.

People generally look at things a certain way — by the outward appearance. In First Samuel 16:7, God told the prophet Samuel that the Lord doesn't see as man sees; for man looks at the outward appearance, but the Lord looks at the heart. People tend to believe that what

Personal Notes

they see is true and often do not discern the inward heart condition of a person.

In some African tribes where witchcraft and Satanic powers are prevalent, the people ask the Christian missionaries, "What can your God do for us?" They are used to seeing manifestations and demonstrations by their gods. For generations they have lived their lives based upon what they see their gods do. A Christian missionary entering into that culture must come with the power of God to heal and deliver them. These people must know that the true God will also do something they can see before they ask Him into their hearts and lives.

Another observation concerning culture is that people who embrace a certain culture also raise their children in the same way of living, thinking, and conduct. Thus each generation views their culture as correct, if not superior, to all other cultures.

Potential problems arise when a person who is indoctrinated in one culture suddenly finds themselves thrust into a very different culture. Potential disorientation, conflict, and problems in relating to other people may occur at this point. This is commonly called "culture shock."

Going into another culture as a minister or "change agent" at the direction of God requires proper training and the right tools to do the job. For example, a shepherd has to know and understand sheep and also have the right training and equipment to successfully shepherd a flock of sheep. Here are some suggestions for a person as he goes into another culture to minister the Gospel.

Get as much knowledge beforehand of the culture you are going to be ministering in. There are various books that can help you adjust to the culture you are going to.

If a minister does not approach people with knowledge of who they are and of their way of life, he may be entirely rejected, or at best received in a very limited manner.

Remember your purpose for being there. This will help keep you steady when your emotions are wanting to flip-flop on you. The Apostle Paul stayed focused on his purpose for being in the ministry no matter where he went. This seemed to be one of the keys to his success.

ACTS 26:16,17 (NKJV)

"But rise and stand on your feet; for I [Jesus] **have appeared to you** [Paul] **for this purpose, to make you a minister and a witness both of the things which you have seen and of the things which I will yet reveal to you.**

"I will deliver you from the Jewish people, as well as from the Gentiles, to whom I now send you."

Remember that God has sent you there. Always be conscious that God is for you, and the Holy Spirit living on the inside of you can handle any conflict or problems

Personal Notes

that may occur. As you obey the direction of God for your life, God will also equip you for effective ministry.

Look at the example of the Apostle Paul. He knew God had sent him to the places he went, so he went to those places depending upon the God who sent him.

> **ACTS 22:21 (NKJV)**
> **"Then He said to me, 'Depart, for I will send you far from here to the Gentiles.'"**

> **1 CORINTHIANS 2:1-5 (NKJV)**
> **And I, brethren, when I came to you, did not come with excellence of speech or of wisdom declaring to you the testimony of God.**
> **For I determined not to know anything among you except Jesus Christ and Him crucified.**
> **I was with you in weakness, in fear, and in much trembling.**
> **And my speech and my preaching were not with persuasive words of human wisdom, but in demonstration of the Spirit and of power,**
> **that your faith should not be in the wisdom of men but in the power of God.**

Recognize the equality of all mankind in God's eyes. There is no difference among mankind from God's perspective. The tendency of mankind is to look on the outward appearance and see the differences that exist, but the Bible tells us there is partiality with God (Rom. 2:11).

GALATIANS 3:28,29 (NKJV)
There is neither Jew nor Greek, there is neither slave nor free, there is neither male nor female; for you are all one in Christ Jesus.
And if you are Christ's, then you are Abraham's seed, and heirs according to the promise.

Let the compassion of Christ move you to minister to people. God's love has been extended to every person, no matter what culture each person may be living in.

JOHN 13:34,35 (NKJV)
"A new commandment I [Jesus] give to you, that you love one another; as I have loved you, that you also love one another.
"By this all will know that you are My disciples, if you have love for one another."

CONCLUSION

Observing culture can help pave the way for the Gospel to be preached effectively. Going to various churches, a traveling minister will find that the people will respond to the message better as he makes an effort to relate to them culturally.

Personal Notes

Special Kinds of Traveling Ministry

33

Traveling Internationally

When a person from the United States travels as a tourist to another country, he often finds himself in a different culture and climate. It is no different for a minister. Therefore a minister who travels internationally is on a different level of the traveling ministry. International travel is different than traveling in America. It requires a different approach, different equipment, and dealing with different cultures, but you must still preach the same Gospel of Jesus Christ.

Sooner or later, many traveling ministers go to a foreign country. God will use anyone who will make himself available. He will use anyone who is willing.

_____

_____

_____

_____

_____

_____

_____

_____

_____

_____

_____

_____

_____

_____

_____

_____

MARK 16:15
And he [Jesus] **said unto them, Go ye into all the world, and preach the gospel to every creature.**

Traveling internationally will help to increase the level of compassion you have for people, and it will add a capacity within you to minister effectively to more people. According to Jesus' words in Mark 16:15, we are to go into all the world and preach the Gospel to every creature. We are to reach every people group with the message of Christ. This is necessary to fulfill the Great Commission of Jesus Christ, and it is a high priority in the heart of God.

In His day, Jesus commented, "...The harvest truly is great, but the labourers are few: pray ye therefore the Lord of the harvest, that he would send forth labourers into his harvest" (Luke 10:2). The harvest is still great today. More people are being saved daily than at any time in the history of the Church. But there is still much work to be done in reaching people with the message of Jesus Christ.

As a traveling minister, Paul traveled to various countries endeavoring to carry the message of Christ to every people group that he could. He reveals his perspective or philosophy of ministry in Romans 1:15-17: "So, as much as in me is, I am ready to preach the gospel to you that are at Rome also. For I am not ashamed of the gospel of Christ: for it is the power of God unto salvation to every one that believeth; to the Jew first, and also to the Greek. For therein is the righteousness of God revealed from faith to faith: as it is written, The just shall live by faith."

Ask yourself this question: Am I sent, or am I just going? When God sends you, you are going in God's timing.

When you are sent at the direction of the Holy Spirit, then you know God will provide.

You must determine if the thrust of your ministry is to go overseas or to minister primarily in the United States. Some traveling ministers are called to travel to foreign countries more than others are. Dr. Lester Sumrall said, "My duty is to tell the untold millions who are yet untold of the grace of God and mercy of Jesus Christ. That is the mandate of every Christian." T. L. Osborn, another great soul winner said, "There is no fulfillment like being part of God's number-one job, sharing the gospel and winning souls — out amidst a suffering world of human persons who need our witness, our touch, our ear, our attention."

GETTING READY TO TRAVEL ABROAD

When preparing to travel abroad, allow plenty of planning time. Usually thirty days to six months is necessary. There are international traveling experts who can help you plan your trip, answer any questions you may have, and obtain airline tickets for you. Some travel agencies that can help you with your needs for international travel include:

MTS Travel, Inc. (various locations)

Bloomfield, NJ	1-800-526-6278
Monroe, WA	1-800-984-9991
Claremont, CA	1-800-854-7979
Colorado Springs, CO	1-800-444-4514
Jacksonville, FL	1-800-888-8292

Personal Notes

Personal Notes

_____

_____

_____

_____

_____

_____

_____

_____

_____

_____

_____

_____

_____

_____

_____

_____

_____

_____

_____

_____

_____

Raptim International Travel

1-800-777-9232 or 716-754-9232

Missionary Advocates for Travel Solutions

704-843-1199

Getting your passport is not difficult. You should allow plenty of time to apply for your passport before you want to travel. It takes anywhere from several weeks to two months to receive your passport, depending upon the time of year you apply. If you are eighteen years of age or older, a passport is valid for ten years from the day it is issued. And a passport is valid for five years for those under eighteen years of age.

1. Applications for passports can be obtained at the county courthouse and at some U.S. Post Offices. The application will have instructions on the back side.

2. Along with your application, proof of U.S. citizenship is necessary — usually a certified copy of your birth certificate.

3. You will need two pictures of yourself to accompany the application. They may be obtained at various places, including some travel agencies.

4. Those 18 years of age or older must submit $65 with their application ($55 passport fee plus a $10 execution fee).

   Those under 18 years of age must submit $40 with their application ($30 passport fee plus $10 execution fee).

Visas are necessary when traveling to certain coun-tries. A visa is an authorization stamped within the passport allowing you to travel in a country for specific purposes and during specific dates.

1. To find out if you need a visa to the country where you are going, contact your travel agency, or the country's embassy or consulate in the United States.

2. If you are short on time, you may need to con-tact someone who knows how to expedite the visa process. First, contact your travel agency to help you. If they cannot help you, contact one (or both) of the companies listed below. Generally, these companies will charge a fee for their services.

Travel Document Systems

1-800-424-8472

American Visa Service

Chicago, IL

312-922-8860

Ask your travel agent about the insurance necessary for your trip. Things you should ask your travel agent about include:

1. Insurance against trip cancellation or interrup-tions, baggage loss, etc.

2. Insurance for medical expenses abroad if you become ill or injured. Medicare does not pay for

Personal Notes

_____

_____

_____

_____

_____

_____

_____

_____

_____

_____

_____

_____

_____

_____

_____

_____

"My duty is to tell the untold millions who are yet untold of the grace of God and mercy of Jesus Christ. That is the mandate of every Christian."

Dr. Lester Sumrall

hospital and medical services outside the United States. You should have other provisions made instead.

4. Insurance for automobile coverage while driving in a foreign country.

5. Additional life insurance.

6. An international driver's license while abroad. An alternative is to hire a national to drive you wherever you need to go.

7. Reimbursement for the flight tickets in case you have to shorten your trip due to an emergency.

How will you raise the money to go to other countries? There are many ways to do this. Some ministers send out a letter to all their supporters and friends asking for donations. Some traveling ministers, during the course of a week-long meeting at a church, will designate one evening's offering toward the missions trip. Some sell items to get the money. Whatever method you choose, you must still:

1. Trust God that He will provide.

2. Have a plan or strategy from God on how to obtain the money.

3. Work the plan until you have the money.

Get information about the countries to which you are traveling. Good sources for information include <u>National Geographic</u> magazine, your local library, or the

LUKE 10:2
Therefore said he unto them, The harvest truly is great, but the labourers are few: pray ye therefore the Lord of the harvest, that he would send forth labourers into his harvest.

Internet. You can find all kinds of information on weather conditions, the political climate, cultural issues, and current events on the Internet.

Learning some basic words of the language of the country you're traveling to is one way to show the nationals you really care about them. Being able to speak words and phrases like "hello," "thank you," "God bless you," or "good-bye" in the language of the people you're ministering to will give you a good report with them and may open doors for you to share Christ with them.

The need for medical care, medicines, and immunizations should be carefully checked out before you go abroad. Some countries require that you to have a certificate of vaccination before they let you enter the country. Ask your local health department or travel agency what you may need. Or you may call:

Centers For Disease Control
Atlanta, Georgia
404-639-2572

Here are some additional traveling tips concerning medical issues.

1. Do not pack all your medicine and prescription drugs in your suitcase, which can get lost or stolen. Keep them in a carry-on bag with you.
2. Always keep your medicine in the original containers to lessen the question of the contents.
3. If you are allergic to certain medications or insect bites, wear a medical bracelet and also keep a

Personal Notes

note in your wallet listing all allergies. Always be sure to carry a card stating your blood type.

4. Check with your doctor or foreign embassies to make sure the prescription drugs you are taking along do not violate the laws of the countries you are traveling to. Do not take a chance of being arrested or denied entrance into the country for having prescription drugs on you. You may need to obtain a certificate from your doctor stating that you need these prescription drugs. However, even that may not be enough authorization to get them into certain countries.

5. If you are wearing eyeglasses or contact lenses, bring along an extra pair along with lens solution and cleaner. Another item to carry is a small eyeglass repair kit.

6. If you become seriously injured or ill, a U.S. Consular officer can help you find the necessary medical help. Generally, help can be found at the U.S. Embassies located in countries throughout the world.

Travel items that you may find useful in traveling internationally can be found at various stores, such as Rand McNally stores, Sears, etc. Several catalogs that may be helpful to you because they are filled with travel items and advice include:

Magellan's

110 W. Sola Street

Santa Barbara, CA 93101-3007

1-800-962-4943

www.magellans.com

Travel Smith

60 Leveroni Crt., Suite 109

Novato, CO 94949

1-800-950-1600

www.travelsmith.com

DEALING WITH OTHER COUNTRIES AND CULTURES

Inquire about the laws of foreign countries you are traveling to, especially local ordinances in the city or area where you want to minister.

Getting your money exchanged for foreign currency is an issue you need to deal with as soon as you enter a country. Here are some suggestions.

1. Try to deal only with authorized outlets such as banks and hotels. Airports usually have higher exchange rates. You may find it necessary to shop around for the best exchange rate.

2. Exchange only the amount of money that you think you will use while you are in a country,

Personal Notes

_____

_____

_____

_____

_____

_____

_____

_____

_____

_____

_____

_____

_____

_____

_____

_____

_____

_____

"God will use anybody who will make himself (or herself) available. He will use anyone who is willing."

Jerry Savelle

Personal Notes

_____

_____

_____

_____

_____

_____

_____

_____

_____

_____

_____

_____

_____

ACTS 1:8
But ye shall receive power,
after that the Holy Ghost is
come upon you: and ye shall
be witnesses unto me both
in Jerusalem, and in all
Judaea, and in Samaria,
and unto the uttermost part
of the earth.

because some countries do not allow you to exchange it back into American dollars.

3. Resist using the black market to get your money exchanged at a lower rate. It is not a legal way of doing business in foreign countries.

Store your passports in the hotel in which you are staying, preferably in the hotel vault. This is especially important when staying in a larger city. Passports may be needed to exchange money; otherwise do not carry them. American passports are worth a lot of money on the black market. In some countries Americans may get mugged or killed because someone wants their passport.

If your passport, money, or traveler's checks are stolen or lost, immediately contact the local police. You should also apply for a replacement passport at the nearest U.S. Embassy or Consulate as soon as possible. If you lose your credit cards, immediately contact the companies who issued the cards to you.

Here are some tips when staying in a hotel while abroad:

1. Request a room between the second and seventh floor. This prevents easy access from outside, while still allowing access to fire escapes in case of a fire.

2. Always meet your visitors in the lobby of the hotel instead of in your room.

3. Never give out your room number to others.

4. Always keep your doors and windows locked.

5. Always leave and enter by the front entrance. Be observant and on guard in the parking lot and nearby vicinity.

Do not go out alone, especially after dark. Always let someone know where you are going and an approximate time you expect to return. Crime is rampant in many countries, so do not make yourself a vulnerable target for attack. Avoid shortcuts, dark alleys, and poorly-lit streets.

Avoid being alone. In some countries it is not safe to be alone in a city even in broad daylight. It is best to always travel with a local person or another team member whenever you travel throughout a foreign country.

Avoid a taxi that picks up more than one client per cab. Use taxi service from the airport or hotel. If the cab has no meter, always agree to the fare in advance.

Choose food over extra clothes in packing for your trip. Tupperware containers that hold ten to fifteen pounds of snacks, canned meats, coffee, etc. are ideal to take along. When traveling in the tropics, be sure to take salt with you.

Drinking water may be a problem where you are traveling. Most water problems are bacteria related, so take some pills along to kill the bacteria in the water. In

Personal Notes

Personal Notes

_____
_____
_____
_____
_____
_____
_____
_____
_____
_____
_____
_____

"There is no fulfillment like being part of God's number-one job, sharing the gospel and winning souls — out amidst a suffering world of human persons who need our witness, our touch, our ear, our attention."

T.L. Osborn

some situations you can mix one teaspoon of bleach to ten quarts of water to make it safe to drink. Drink coffee or soda pop when possible.

Miscellaneous tips:

1. Preparation H can be used on insect bites to relieve soreness and swelling.
2. Chigger Guard is a good thing to take along, especially in warmer countries.
3. Always wear appropriate clothes for the climate you are going to. For example, wear pants with tight pant legs when traveling in the jungle, so nothing can crawl under your pant leg.

When making purchases in foreign countries, keep in mind the customs and duty laws. You are allowed to bring four hundred dollars' worth of goods into America before customs apply. Certain items may be illegal to take out of the country you visited or illegal to bring into the States. So check the laws before buying items.

For more information in traveling abroad you may write to:

Americans Abroad
Consumer Information Center
Pueblo, CO 81009

PREACHING THE GOSPEL IN OTHER COUNTRIES

In setting up your ministry schedule, always try to be specific with your contact abroad. Find out what ministry opportunities are available, and let your contact know what you can or are willing to do. Try to have an established ministry schedule set up for you before you leave home. Often it is easier to have a local contact put together an itinerary for you in the country you are traveling to.

Last-minute changes may happen, so be prepared to be flexible once you arrive. Your primary objective is to serve and show the love of God to the people. Be a servant of Christ as much as possible to your host and to the people.

Be sensitive to the people's culture. Breaking cultural rules and protocol may hinder the people from receiving the Gospel from you. Ask your contact to instruct you on things concerning the culture that you need to know. When possible, flow with the church's wants, customs, and traditions.

You can access a lot of helpful information in how to relate properly to cultures in more than sixty countries from Terri Morrison's book <u>Kiss, Bow, or Shake Hands</u>. This book provides cultural insights, information on how to conduct business, and protocol on a number of issues.

Personal Notes

_____

_____

_____

_____

_____

_____

_____

_____

_____

_____

ROMANS 1:15-17
So, as much as in me is, I am ready to preach the gospel to you that are at Rome also. For I am not ashamed of the gospel of Christ: for it is the power of God unto salvation to every one that believeth; to the Jew first, and also to the Greek.
For therein is the righteousness of God revealed from faith to faith: as it is written, The just shall live by faith.

It also includes lists of various issues or gestures that may be offensive to people in various countries.

Preach the Word of God. Declare the Gospel is the power of God to people. Do not compromise the Gospel with the people on the issue of salvation. You are there to preach salvation. On matters other than salvation, try to be as flexible as possible. Realize those people will change as they receive understanding of the Word of God. You can not force change on people on a short-term basis. It takes time for people to grow in the Lord.

1. Avoid addressing customs and traditions.
2. Do not try to "Americanize" the people. Lead the people to Christ, but also let them be who they are in their culture.
3. Be prepared to minister healing by the power of God and deal with evil spirits if necessary.

CONCLUSION

We must adopt the same attitude Paul stated that he had so we may be effective ministers worldwide.

1 CORINTHIANS 9:18-22
What is my reward then? Verily that, when I preach the gospel, I may make the gospel of Christ without charge, that I abuse not my power in the gospel.
For though I be free from all men, yet have I made myself servant unto all, that I might gain the more.

And unto the Jews I became as a Jew, that I might gain the Jews; to them that are under the law, as under the law, that I might gain them that are under the law;

To them that are without law, as without law, (being not without law to God, but under the law to Christ,) that I might gain them that are without law.

To the weak became I as weak, that I might gain the weak: I am made all things to all men, that I might by all means save some.

Personal Notes

34

Traveling Children's Ministry

Traveling ministers whose primary focus is ministering to children are a very vital and important part of ministry. They are helping to set the course the children will later travel. It is probably impossible to count how many people can trace their first experience with God back to attending a children's camp or a special service where a guest speaker gave the invitation for children to accept Christ as their Saviour. Statistics reveal that most people who accept Christ do so before the age of eighteen, and most of them do so as children.

Some people do not recognize the importance of touching children's lives with the Gospel of Jesus Christ.

Personal Notes

It's been said that if we paid no more attention to our plants than we have to our children, we would now be living in a jungle of weeds. The Scriptures tell us to "train up a child in the way he should go: and when he is old, he will not depart from it" (Prov. 22:6). If we want the next generation to serve God, we must make every effort to reach them while they are still children.

Observe Jesus' attitude toward children: "...Suffer the little children to come unto me, and forbid them not: for of such is the kingdom of God (Mark 10:14). His attitude was to welcome the children, and He stopped what He was doing to spend time ministering to them.

One possible reason that children are often overlooked is because traveling ministers may be looking for the recognition of ministering in adult services. However, children are often more receptive to the Gospel than adults. They exhibit a readiness to believe the Word of God that adults cannot or do not show.

PREPARING FOR YOUR CHILDREN'S MEETINGS

You may want to have introductory information about your ministry. This may include:

1. Plenty of pictures of ministering to children.
2. References and credentials clearly stated.
3. Information stating your track record and how long you've been in the traveling children's ministry.

PROVERBS 22:6
Train up a child in the way he should go: and when he is old, he will not depart from it.

Doing the above helps build a security factor in the minds of those who want to bring you into their church to minister to their children.

It will help you know how to be more effective if you find out what the pastor's objective is in having an outside children's minister come into his church. His objective may be to provide relief for the local children's workers and to include them in the special meetings, to boost the church's image in the community, or to train the local children's workers.

Here are some questions you can ask when scheduling a meeting in a local church:

1. What kind of meetings do they want?
2. How many meetings do they want you to do?
3. What is their normal procedure in children's ministry?
4. How long should the service last?

You may want to obtain a doctrinal statement from the pastor if you are not familiar with him or the church. You should make every effort to be in agreement with pastor and avoid controversial issues.

Ask about the children's ministry equipment that the church has available in the church. Finding out the age of their existing equipment will give you an idea as to the quality of the equipment and whether or not you can use it for your programs.

Personal Notes

_____

_____

_____

_____

_____

_____

_____

_____

_____

_____

_____

_____

_____

_____

_____

"Those who educate children well are more to be honored than they who produce them; for these only gave them life, those the art of living well."

Aristotle

Financial needs should be discussed ahead of time. You may need to communicate clearly what your expenses are, including travel, lodging, meals, etc., and get an agreement from the church to cover those expenses. As a traveling children's minister, you will normally have more equipment and supplies to take along than most other traveling ministers, so asking for your expenses to be reimbursed is not unreasonable.

Decide whether or not you will be bringing your own equipment, costumes, puppets and puppet stage, object lessons, supplies, and prizes, etc. You will also need to provide a list to the church stating what still needs to be provided for children's ministry.

Try to develop your ministry options so that you can be as versatile as possible. Sometimes churches want more than just a children's minister. Sometimes they also want you to train their children's church staff or to minister in an adult meeting. Be open to what the pastor may want.

CONDUCTING YOUR CHILDREN'S MEETINGS

Bringing your own equipment will be necessary at times. In fact, you may find that you prefer to do that all the time. Here is a partial list of equipment that you might consider:

1. Costumes — your choices can include biblical, animal, or cartoon characters, etc.
2. Various puppets and a portable puppet stage.
3. Music and puppet accompaniment tapes.
4. Object lessons and supplies.
5. Prizes — candy, inexpensive items, etc.
6. Construction equipment — construction and art supplies, light hand tools, etc.
7. Special lighting — an overhead projector may be used to show song transparencies and for spot lighting as necessary.
8. A van or trailer to haul your equipment when you travel.

Your ministry emphasis is to change peoples' lives for the glory of God!

1. It should not be just entertainment, although what you do may be entertaining.
2. Seeing God move and minister to the children should be your goal. Whatever happens to adults can happen to children. Manifestations of the Holy Ghost can happen in children's services also, usually in a more pure form than in an adult atmosphere. Often children are not as inhibited as adults are, and their intellect does not hinder them from acting in faith as much as adult's intellect might.
3. It is not the method, but the message that is important.

Personal Notes

_____

_____

_____

_____

_____

_____

_____

_____

_____

_____

_____

_____

_____

_____

_____

_____

_____

_____

_____

"Every child born into the world is a new thought of God, an ever-fresh and radiant possibility."

Kate Douglas Wiggin

The question of whether to hold the meeting indoors or outdoors depends on various things, such as the condition of the tent, weather, security for your equipment, etc. Each situation is different, so you have to evaluate each one on its own positives and negatives. Make sure your equipment is secure. You may have to communicate this ahead of time, so the church can make the necessary accommodations for you.

Dealing with children and their parents can be a very touchy matter. Parents are concerned about their children and want to be assured of their well-being and safety. As a children's minister, you have the opportunity to minister God's love to people through taking good care of their children.

1. Use positive incentives with the children to encourage good behavior and participation in the services. For example, announce at the beginning of your meeting that there will be a "quiet-seat" prize for the child who behaved the best during the service.

2. Another good technique is to have prize drawings during times when the children are behaving well. This motivates and rewards the children at the right time. Connect the reward with the performance if at all possible.

3. Be aware that various things can cause a child to become a problem or behave badly. Here are some things to look for:
   - The room condition, i.e. crowded, hot, etc.
   - Conflict with a worker — some personalities just do not get along. You may have to let the worker do something else.
   - The child may be on medication that makes him behave a certain way.
   - A child may have ALDS — Acquired Learning Disability Syndrome
   - The child may come from a dysfunctional family.

4. The time length, methods, and teaching concepts of each activity in your meetings should be adjusted to the attention span of the age group you're ministering to. You can figure approximately one minute per year of the child's age in determining the attention span of children. For younger children, use faster and more simple presentations. Check the length of your session time. Be sure to move from one activity to the next fairly rapidly.

5. Do not allow one child to dominate your class or take all your time. You may have to deal with a child openly if his behavior is severe enough.

Personal Notes

_____

_____

_____

_____

_____

_____

_____

_____

_____

_____

_____

_____

_____

_____

_____

_____

_____

"If we paid no more attention to our plants than we have to our children, we would now be living in a jungle of weeds."

(Unknown)

_____

_____

_____

_____

_____

_____

_____

_____

_____

_____

_____

_____

_____

_____

_____

_____

_____

LUKE 9:48
. . .Whosoever shall receive this child in my name receiveth me: and whosoever shall receive me receiveth him that sent me: for he that is least among you all, the same shall be great.

Removal from the children's ministry area should be the most extreme discipline to use.

6. Honest communication with the children's parents is a must. Tell the parents about the children's conduct and solicit their help and ideas in ministering to the children.

Security is an issue with parents when you are ministering to their children. Because of things that have happened to children in various places in the past, you may consider getting liability insurance. Here are some guidelines in conducting your children's meetings that may help you from being held liable.

1. Do not conduct children's meetings by yourself. Request a helper so you have a witness that can verify what actually takes place in your meetings.

2. Always have two workers in the prayer room, or do your ministering openly where it can be seen by everyone.

3. Know those who labor among you. Do not allow every volunteer to help. If you do not know anyone personally where you're ministering, use only those recommended by the local church leadership.

Following up with the children who receive Christ and are filled with the Spirit in your meetings is necessary. Get their names and addresses and give them to the local church, so they can be visited and encouraged to come back to church. Remember, if you follow a child home, you'll find a family there. So reaching the whole family is very possible through children's ministry.

Keeping records of what happened in each place you ministered is a good idea. Here are some things to keep records of:

1. What you taught
2. The number of children in attendance
3. The number of children who received salvation, baptism with the Holy Spirit, etc.
4. Outstanding special events that occurred in the meetings
5. The income you received
6. Your book table sales (if you have one)
7. The pastor's name and his children's names

ETHICAL ISSUES IN MINISTERING TO CHILDREN

It may be a wise to get experience in children's ministry in a local church before entering into a traveling children's ministry. This will help you know what children's ministers are facing and how to best minister to children. Also, this will give you credibility in the minds of other church leaders when they want someone to come in and minister to their children.

Personal Notes

Personal Notes

As a traveling children's minister, you will find it beneficial to have a confidant. It may be wise to have a pastor fill this role if possible. He can share many things from a local church viewpoint that others couldn't.

Never allow yourself to become isolated. Avoid getting into the "Elijah syndrome," thinking you are all alone. That is a trap of the enemy to snare you and cause you to fail in your ministry. Put forth the effort to search out new friends.

Make sure you are ministering for the glory of God. Make up your mind that you want God to commend you and that you are not going to depend upon man for your approval.

Do not get upset if you do not receive the respect of the pastor in the churches you go to. Many times as a children's minister you will not be received as an equal in ministry by those who minister to the adults. At times you may not be included in fellowship times with other ministers, and you may become very lonely. This is not right, but to stay effective in ministry, you have to learn to overlook it.

1. You can not concentrate on what is fair or unfair. Remember your call is from God, not man.

2. Decide to become better, not bitter. Remember, God is doing the counting that matters in the end.

MARK 10:14
...Suffer the little children to come unto me, and forbid them not: for of such is the kingdom of God.

3. Determine to walk in love. In doing so you are expressing the character of God to those around you. This can convict the other ministers, and may cause them to include you in their fellowship.

Remember that even though you are traveling, you still need a home church base and need to be submitted to a pastor. This is scriptural, and it will also give you credibility with other churches where you go to minister. It will certainly contribute to your spiritual well-being.

Make sure you communicate openly with the pastor so that no misunderstandings will develop between you while you are there. Sometimes pastors get busy, so it is up to you to put forth the effort to communicate with them.

CONCLUSION

As a children's minister, you have the opportunity to minister to many who have the potential of becoming great people in their lifetime. Remember what Jesus said Luke 9:48, "...Whosoever shall receive this child in my name receiveth me: and whosoever shall receive me receiveth him that sent me: for he that is least among you all, the same shall be great."

When you are looking at the children in front of you, remember what they might become. As Kate Douglas Wiggin said, "Every child born into the world is

Personal Notes

Personal Notes

a new thought of God, an ever-fresh and radiant possibility." And Aristotle, the famous Greek philosopher, said, "Those who educate children well are more to be honored than they who produce them; for these only gave them life, those the art of living well."

35

Women in the Traveling Ministry

Today there are many women ministers who are very effective and successful in their ministries. They do not make an issue of being a woman minister or of the prejudices that they sometimes encounter. They simply rely on God to make a place for them to minister, and they rely on the anointing to help them. They have wonderful ministries that effectively minister to the needs of the people and touch people's lives positively for Jesus Christ.

On the other hand, there are also women ministers who continually make a big issue of being a woman in the ministry and make an issue of the prejudices they have

PROVERBS 18:16

A man's [and a woman's] gift maketh room for him, and bringeth him before great men....

PROVERBS 17:8

A gift is as a precious stone in the eyes of him that hath it: whithersoever it turneth, it prospereth.

Personal Notes

_____

_____

_____

_____

_____

_____

_____

_____

_____

_____

_____

experienced from their male colleagues. They are always ready to confront others, especially men, to see what their opinion is about women in ministry. It is sad to say that these women, although they may have been called of God and gifted to minister, are limited in what they can accomplish and have not been very effective in the ministry.

The main difference between successful and unsuccessful women ministers is their attitude. The successful women ministers are trusting God, walking in love, and are secure in their call into the ministry. Unsuccessful women ministers may never have settled the issue of being secure in their call into the ministry, so they concentrate on the things that are wrong in the church and are confrontational rather than offering encouragement and comfort to people.

It is true that women ministers may encounter prejudice and opposition simply because they are women. Prejudice, although it is never right, is often a result of things that have been taught in churches throughout the years and a result of ignorance of God's Word.

Throughout the history of the Church, many arguments have been fought over whether women should be allowed to do anything in the ministry. In the final analysis, the whole counsel of God's Word makes it clear that God will use whoever is available to minister to the needs of people.

REMEMBER WHO CALLED YOU INTO THE MINISTRY

Being secure in the fact that God has called you into the ministry is an issue that a woman must deal with when entering into the ministry, especially the traveling ministry. Insecurity in this area can affect your attitude toward others and affect how you respond to ministers around you. It can also cause you to attempt to evaluate your true worth by comparing yourself with others instead of by what the Bible says about you. Here are some things that can help you settle the "security issue" in ministry.

Yes   No

☐   ☐   Is there a definitive moment when God called you into the ministry that you can use as a reference point? Explain.

_____

_____

_____

What scriptures will support you as a woman in ministry? Your selection of scriptures should deal specifically with women as ministers, not just with women as Christians.

_____

_____

_____

Personal Notes

Personal Notes

_____
_____
_____
_____
_____
_____
_____
_____
_____
_____
_____
_____
_____
_____
_____
_____
_____
_____

Yes   No

☐   ☐   Are there other ministers who believe in you as a minister and in the ministry that God has called you to? Name them.

_____

_____

_____

Yes   No

☐   ☐   Do you need to stop attempting to establish your true worth by comparing yourself with other ministers? Explain.

_____

_____

_____

The ministry is a male-dominated profession, and prejudice in the church world against women ministers does exist. Although that is not right, if you are a woman, you will probably need to prepare for it. Here are some things that can help you be ready if you encounter opposition as a minister due to the fact you are a woman.

1. Do not make a big issue about the prejudice you encounter or start a crusade against it. Let God vindicate you.

2. Do not say anything at the expense of the pastor, especially while you are in the pulpit. Do not attack

men or their prejudices. It would take a definite word from God and a very strong anointing to address this successfully.

3. Realize that God has deposited gifts inside you to equip you for ministry. If you will begin to use the gifts that God has given you, they will make room for you and create opportunities for you to minister the Gospel. No matter what man, the devil, or circumstances say, God will use your gifts to cause you to prosper in your ministry.

4. Do not make a big issue about being a woman. God uses both men and women. Rely upon the call of God that you have received, letting that speak for itself.

5. Trust God for favor with every person you deal with. God can prepare people's hearts and cause them to deal favorably with you. Expect the favor of God to make a way for you.

6. Walk in love. Do not let another person's actions determine the quality of your Christian walk and your ministry.

7. Rely upon the scriptures that tell you God has called you. Trust God to show you His perfect will for you and to give you a vision for the ministry He has for you.

Personal Notes

SAFEGUARDING YOURSELF IN THE MINISTRY

As a woman in the traveling ministry, you will go to many different places and find yourself in many different situations. Ask God to give you wisdom to deal effectively with the problems you may encounter. Be alert and make every effort to avoid potentially dangerous or compromising situations.

Whether in a hotel or in a church, you must be prepared to deal with issues or situations that have the potential of being dangerous or destroying your ministry. Here are some safeguards to help you deal with these types of issues and situations.

1. If possible, do not travel alone. As much as possible, have either your husband or another female travel with you.

2. If possible, try to do your traveling in the daytime, especially when you are driving to your meetings.

3. Ask to stay in hotel rooms that are in the front part of the hotel. Avoid the back areas of the hotel where prowlers may access the hotel unnoticed. Sometimes it is better to spend a few more dollars for a better hotel room.

4. Avoid being alone with a minister or person of the opposite sex as much as possible. If you do find yourself alone, here are some options:

- Ask another person to come into the room as soon as possible.
- Try to get where other people are as soon as possible.
- Keep some distance between yourself and the other minister.
- If necessary, keep a desk or a piece of furniture between you and the other minister.

5. Here are some guidelines to help you in dealing with potentially compromising situations with ministers of the opposite sex.

- Avoid all appearances of evil. Some situations may not be wrong in themselves, but to other people they may not look good. This gives room for gossip and rumors to start.
- Avoid temptation at all costs. This means avoiding situations which may be a temptation to you and avoiding situations where others might be tempted.
- Be careful about any physical contact between you and ministers of the opposite sex, such as hugs or standing so close together that your bodies touch one another. Often a simple handshake while greeting another minister is sufficient. If you do give another minister a hug do it in such a way that no physical contact occurs below the shoulders.

Personal Notes

Personal Notes

- Avoid situations that make you uncomfortable as a person.
- If meeting with a minister of the opposite sex is unavoidable, suggest that you meet in an open, public area around other people. Avoid meeting behind closed doors.
- Avoid going to lunch alone with the pastor. Make sure the pastor's wife or at least another person, such as the associate pastor, is also going along.
- If a pastor is driving you somewhere such as the airport or to another church, make sure that his wife is also going along. If she cannot, ask if their children or a church member can go along. Do not be afraid to communicate with the pastor if something is not right and you cannot go along with it.
- Include the pastor's wife in planning events while at a church. This creates good will and helps avoid having your intentions misread.

POSITIVE, SCRIPTURAL GUIDELINES FOR SUCCESSFUL MINISTRY

In the final analysis, the Body of Christ needs to hear from women ministers. Often a man cannot speak in such a way that a woman can relate to his message, and male ministers also need to hear the perspective of a woman in order to maintain a balanced and comprehensive ministry to women sitting under their own ministry.

As a woman in the traveling ministry, remember the following guidelines for successful ministry.

1. Realize you are a valuable gift to the Church. Do not let anyone convince you otherwise.

2. Concentrate on preaching the Word of God. God has promised to confirm His Word that is preached — not personal crusades or pet topics.

3. Be bold in speaking the Word, but at the same time realize that as a woman your gifts include gentleness and sensitivity. The church needs to hear from a woman's perspective in dealing with its problems. But remember that being bold is not the same as being arrogant, domineering, or condemning.

4. Use common sense in dealing with the natural things of the ministry, such as accounting, booking meetings, and financial matters. Do not try to spiritualize everything or receive a word from the Lord on every detail.

5. Be patient. Give your ministry time to bear godly fruit, and then your well-doing will hush the mouths of your critics. They cannot argue with the fruit your ministry bears. Let God defend you. You are simply instructed to be faithful to His call.

Personal Notes

6. Learn to utilize the advice, counsel, and wisdom of men, both businessmen and ministers, who believe in your ministry and support you. Sometimes a woman's perspective needs to be balanced by a man's viewpoint and vice versa. Proverbs 24:6 tells us that "...by wise counsel thou shalt make thy war: and in multitude of counsellors there is safety." There are certain situations that would be better for a man to deal with, such as counseling men, visiting men in the hospital, etc. Use wisdom when deciding your course of action in any situation.

CONCLUSION

God will put men and women in the Body of Christ as it pleases Him. As you learn to function in your place and calling, you will please God, and His favor will be upon your ministry. Whether a man or a woman, there is a place for you in the Body of Christ, and God will equip you for successful ministry.

36

Conducting Your Own Meetings

There are various reasons why traveling ministers will conduct their own meetings in a neutral place such as a hotel room or a civic center. Perhaps it is an effort to fulfill the call of God on their life. It could be an attempt to reach people who would not come to a church. It could be to obey the Great Commission of Jesus Christ in Matthew 28:1: "Go ye therefore, and teach ALL nations...." It could also be the united effort of local churches and ministries to have special meetings to reach the community for Christ.

You must know why you are conducting a meeting in a neutral place. Having a purpose will help you concentrate your efforts and finances effectively in order to maximize the

Personal Notes

_____

_____

_____

_____

_____

_____

_____

_____

_____

_____

_____

_____

_____

ministry that takes place in your meeting. Your purpose will determine what kind of meeting your are going to have, such as a crusade, seminar, revival, etc.

PREPARING TO CONDUCT YOUR OWN CRUSADE MEETINGS

In conducting meetings in a neutral place, your goal should be to reach as many people as possible. Therefore you should make every effort to remove every hindrance that would keep people from coming. Consider the following things in selecting dates and places to hold your meetings:

1. A rule of thumb: "North in the summer and south in the winter, unless God tells you otherwise" (Roy Cragg).

2. Consider the weather conditions and the climate. Attendance will be better during suitable weather.

3. Consider the seasonal activities in the area you want to hold meetings. Avoid dates conflicting with city or community events.

4. Consider other Christian events in the area. Avoid creating a conflict of interest, which can affect the attendance to your meetings.

5. Consider holidays. Do not schedule your meetings around holidays.

6. Consider having your meetings in the geographical areas where you are known, especially when you are just starting to conduct your own meetings.

Getting a facility that will meet the needs of the meeting will be your responsibility. Here are some things to consider in getting a facility for your meetings. These factors will influence people to either attend or not attend your meeting.

1. The type of meeting you want will determine the type of facility you need.

2. Get a local contact person if possible. They can do things and check things out locally that you cannot do from your office.

3. Attendance will determine the size of the facility you need. Be conservative in your estimates of what you will need. Remember that a full room creates a better atmosphere than a room that is only half full.

4. Some facilities may require you to schedule your meetings well in advance or to be flexible on your dates because other events may be scheduled in the same facility.

5. Consider the reputation and condition of the facility. The local people will not come as readily to a building or location that does not have a

Personal Notes

good reputation or is not kept in good condition. Ask questions such as the following:

- Is it in an area of high crime, or in an area of relative safety?
- Is it attractive and clean, and does it have modern facilities in it?
- Is ample parking available?
- Is it easy for people to find? (This is very important.)
- Is it easy to get to, or is it in an area of congested traffic?

6. Consider the financial cost of the facility. You will have to pay for using the facility. Be conservative in your estimation of projected meeting income and expenses. The most economical facility to get is a church building. However, be sure to treat the pastor properly and ethically. You may want to get your agreement with the church in writing so misunderstandings do not develop and you don't lose a friend. Be willing to pay for the use of the building, and flow with what the pastor asks for.

Public facilities are cheaper than hotel ballrooms, because they are often funded by taxes. Check to see if they have different room sizes available. Schools and university facilities are usually fairly reasonable in cost, but they may also be more difficult to rent.

Hotel ballrooms are the most expensive facilities to rent. The hotels do not make their money on the meeting rooms, but in the food and lodging rooms that they sell.

Make sure that all contracts with hotels and the organizations you are dealing with spell out the specific details and arrangements you have agreed to verbally. Be sure to read the whole contract.

Check to see if local labor union workers are required for any loading, unloading, setup, or teardown of your meeting equipment. If they are required, you will have to pay their wages, and it will increase the expenses of your meeting. If you cannot afford this, you may have to get a different facility.

Advertising is another issue that you are responsible for when conducting your own meetings. It is an expense you have to pay for. If you are not experienced in creating advertising or running an ad campaign, you may save money by hiring a professional who has the necessary contacts and can help focus your advertising for better results. Advertising is an up-front expense. Different places to advertise include:

- Your own newsletter or ministry magazine.
- Direct mail letters to individuals and churches in the area.
- Local television and radio.
- Local Christian bookstores.

Personal Notes

Personal Notes

> • Local newspapers (You may want to consider advertising in the entertainment section where non-Christians would also look.)

You will also have to consider the equipment that is necessary to conduct your meetings. Some the equipment that you may need will include:

> • A good public address (PA) system and audio recording equipment.
> • Cassette tapes and tape duplicator.
> • Usher badges, offering buckets and envelopes, and modesty cloths.
> • A podium and possibly your own platform.
> • Book tables and cover cloths.
> • An adding machine and a deposit stamp for the offerings and book table sales.
> • Salvation packets and address cards.
> • Ministry partner packets.

You will have to provide your own music for praise and worship, or have a team with you who can.

> 1. Make sure you know who is going to provide instruments to play the music.
> 2. Local churches are a good source for musicians to help in your crusades. Use your local contact to find them.

Support personnel such as ushers, greeters, helpers, counselors, etc. are some of the help you will need to successfully minister to the people in your meetings.

1. You may be able to get these people through local churches in the area.

2. You will want to have some form of recommendation from local contacts in order to screen your volunteer help. Do not just accept everyone who wants to volunteer.

PROPER ETHICS TOWARD LOCAL PASTORS AND CHURCHES

The real success of your meetings will often be determined by your relationships with local pastors and whether you deal with them in an ethical manner. If the local pastors do not support your meetings, your success will be limited. Here are some suggestions when dealing with the local pastors.

1. Clearly communicate to the pastors your intentions and the purpose for your meeting.

2. Assure the pastors that your meeting is not intended to start another church. NOTE: If you are holding your own meetings in a neutral place to start a church, communicate clearly that this is what you are intending to do.

3. Be ethical in dealing with finances and receiving offerings. Do not resort to gimmicks, prophetic

Personal Notes

Personal Notes

manipulation, etc. to receive more money from the people.

4. Make sure the local pastors get the names of those who receive salvation, so they can follow up with them to invite them to their church.

5. Do not major on controversial or pet doctrines. Preach the Word of God. Make sure that your preaching reflects the whole counsel of God's Word.

CONCLUSION

The next page contains a worksheet that may help you organize your own meetings and produce a budget for the meeting.

Conducting your own crusade meetings takes a lot of planning and organization. If planning and organization are not some of your strong points, you may need to hire someone who is an administrator and well-organized.

Conducting your own meetings is another realm of the traveling ministry. Your approach has to be different, and the responsibility is greater than just traveling from church to church. Be encouraged to do all you can do in reaching the world for Jesus Christ!

Note: Much of the information in this lesson came from "Crusade Organization," a course taught at Rhema Bible Training Center by Rev. Roy Cragg.

MEETING FACILITY WORKSHEET

GENERAL INFORMATION

Location (Address/City/State) _____

Facility name _____ Facility phone # _____

Fax # _____ Contact person _____

Date contacted _____ Dates requested _____

Alternate dates _____ Contract: Accepted ☐ Rejected ☐

FACILITY DATA

Room name _____

Seating capacity_____ Parking capacity _____

Sound equipment provided: Yes No Union workers required: Yes No

Book table area: Yes No Prayer/Counselor area: Yes No

Security provided: Yes No Insurance required: Yes No

MEETING COSTS

Facility costs:$_____(per day) x _____(# days) = $_____

Insurance costs:$ _____

Labor costs:_____ # people x $_____per hr. x____hrs. per day x____# days = $_____

Union costs:_____ # people x $_____per hr. x____hrs. per day x____# days = $_____

Security:$_____per hr. x____# hrs. per day x____# days = $_____

Parking: $_____per day x____# days x____# vehicles = $_____

Advertising costs: (add the items below for this total) $_____

Radio $_____ Newspaper $_____

Television $_____ Direct mail $_____

Posters, etc. $_____ Other $_____

Travel costs: (add the items below for this total) $_____

Airlines: $_____per ticket x_____# people = $_____

$_____per ticket x_____# people = $_____

Fuel for vehicle #1 $_____

Fuel for vehicle #2 $_____

Fuel for vehicle #3 $_____

Food costs: $_____per person x____# people x____# days = $_____

Hotel costs: $_____per person x____# people x____# days = $_____

Misc. costs: (add the items below for this total) $_____

Other _____ $_____

Other _____ $_____

TOTAL MEETING COSTS $_____

37

Traveling Music Ministries

Music can play a vital role in communicating the Gospel. Traveling ministers who offer a singing or music ministry bring a dimension of ministry that often helps people to receive the truth of God's Word into their lives. It can also help a minister flow in the anointing so that he can minister effectively to the people.

Even in the Old Testament we see how music helped the prophet Elisha to operate in his ministry office. Second Kings 3:15 says, "But now bring me a minstrel. And it came to pass, when the minstrel played, that the hand of the Lord came upon him."

2 KINGS 3:15

But now bring me a minstrel. And it came to pass, when the minstrel played, that the hand of the Lord came upon him.

Personal Notes

_____

_____

_____

_____

_____

_____

_____

_____

_____

_____

_____

_____

_____

_____

_____

In John 4:24, God emphasizes that His people should worship Him. The scripture reads, "God is a Spirit: and they that worship him must worship him in spirit and in truth." So we see that the ministry of music is necessary in serving God, and it is also very powerful in ministering to people. However, a powerful tool has to be used correctly and within certain guidelines, or it has the potential of causing a great deal of harm.

CONDUCTING YOUR MEETINGS IN CHURCHES

Communication with the pastor or leaders in the church while you are scheduling your meetings is often necessary so that you can flow together. Here are some guidelines to follow in setting up your meetings.

You must be submitted and flow with the pastor's desires. Be flexible in your ministry requirements because every situation is different. Develop various options so that your ministry can offer something within the requirements of various situations.

Promotional materials can include posters and demo tapes sent to churches as needed. Be sure your demo tape is up to date with what you are currently doing. A nonprofessional demo tape of your latest music is better than a professional music tape recorded ten years ago.

Ask about the public address (PA) equipment in the church you are going to, then evaluate your needs.

You may need to bring more of your own equipment to minister effectively.

1. Most musicians are very particular about what comes through their monitors. However, be careful that you also hear what the audience is hearing, so proper adjustments can be made.

2. An option you may consider to establish consistency in the sound of your music from place to place is to have your own small mixing board, monitors, and speakers on the platform with you and run the sound through a line into the church PA system. The church sound person can set his PA levels and not worry about your sound. You can make the necessary adjustments you need from the platform.

3. Communicate to the pastor what equipment you may need to bring along in order for you to perform your music properly. It is better to communicate this before you get to the church rather than walk in with the equipment when you arrive.

Security is a concern when you have valuable equipment set up to play your music. Make sure the meeting rooms or sanctuary will be locked when no one is there. Take the valuable items that can easily be detached and carry them with you to your hotel room or wherever you are staying.

Personal Notes

JOHN 4:24
God is a Spirit: and they that worship him must worship him in spirit and in truth.

PSALM 150:1-5

Praise ye the Lord. Praise God in his sanctuary: praise him in the firmament of his power.

Praise him for his mighty acts: praise him according to his excellent greatness.

Praise him with the sound of the trumpet: praise him with the psaltery and harp.

Praise him with the timbrel and dance: praise him with stringed instruments and organs.

Praise him upon the loud cymbals: praise him upon the high sounding cymbals.

Working with sound personnel in the local church is a must. They are working with a fixed set of variables and usually know how they want to have the sound in the church. If you need to give them some instructions pertaining to your music, do so tactfully. Ask them to help you face this challenge, and communicate to them that their opinion is important to you.

The physical act of unloading and loading your equipment, sound checks, etc. can wear you out. Plan carefully in this area so that you do not get over involved in the details of equipment setup rather than preparing to minister to the people.

1. If you have a lot of equipment, you may ask the pastor if several people from the congregation could be there to help you unload it. Be sure to be at the church promptly at the time that was agreed upon if you're going to do this.

2. Evaluate what you really need to do in order to minister to the people, not just entertain them. Protect your anointing by prioritizing what you do.

USE WISDOM IN THE CHURCH SERVICES WHERE YOU MINISTER

How you conduct your music in your meetings will influence people to receive or to reject the truth of God's

Word. Not only that, the attitude you display while you are singing will influence the people.

Your goal in every service should be to minister to people, not to entertain them. In order to accomplish this goal, you have to work with the pastor and the sound personnel at the local church where you're conducting your meeting. You may want to communicate with the pastor ahead of time that you desire:

1. Not to be offensive in any way.
2. To be submitted to the pastor while you are there.
3. To flow with the pastor so the audience will be ministered to.

Avoid a "professional musician" attitude. Be friendly and personable to the pastor and the people. In the midst of the pressure of schedules and performances, you must remember that ministering to people is the most important issue. Ministering to people is always more important than having a perfect musical performance. Here are some things that may help in ministering to the people:

1. Be willing to adjust the volume levels of your music if the pastor asks you to.
2. To musicians, music seems more dynamic at certain audio levels, and to lower the volume will, in their opinion, take away from the perform-ance. However, if the audience is turned off by the volume of your music, your message and ministry

Personal Notes

will be ineffective. Try to reach a good medium that is not offensive to the people and is still effective in ministry.

3. Your music needs to have some "punch" to it. The people should be able to feel and experience your music. At some point in the service, your music should reach a crescendo, bringing the people into a high level of worship.

4. Remember that your music should also reach the soulish part of people and minister to their emotions as well as to their hearts.

5. Your music should minister to God, but it should also minister to people, exhorting them to minister to God.

6. Avoid extremes in the volume level of your music. Too loud may be offensive, and too soft may be ineffective in ministry.

If your music is contemporary and somewhat loud, you might suggest to the pastor to warn his people and ask those who do not like their music very loud to sit in the back of the auditorium.

Be sensitive to the needs of the audience. Avoid being inflexible. Try to adapt your music to different situations so that the people can receive it. Having a variety of music will provide you with more opportunities to minister to the people.

ASPIRE TO EXCELLENCE IN YOUR MINISTRY

Endeavor to be disciplined in your personal life and with your time. Effective ministry is often the result of maintaining the right priorities in your personal life. Traveling has a tendency to tempt you to be undisciplined.

Make sure your music is high quality. Produce the best music you can. It is better to do a little with excellence than to do a lot at a mediocre level. You will need to have good quality equipment so it can withstand the strain and stress of traveling and produce the quality of excellence you want.

Make sure your music has a strong Gospel message, so people will be ministered to spiritually and not just entertained.

Writing all of your own music may seem to be a good idea at first, but it will limit you both in the viewpoint it presents and in what you can do.

1. If you are concerned about "performance rights," the key is to communicate with the artist ahead of time. Unless you are reproducing the songs for resale on cassette or CD, most artists will allow you to use their songs if you ask them.

2. Do not be so concerned with being original that you are not genuine. Being genuine is a real key in effective ministry.

Personal Notes

PSALM 149:1
Praise ye the Lord. Sing unto the Lord a new song, and his praise in the congregation of saints.

Personal Notes

Perform all of your music for the glory of God. Remember that you are accountable to God, and He will commend you in the end.

CONCLUSION

Music is a very vital aspect of ministry, and sometimes it is the only way God can get through to a person. At times the music is critical in bringing a preacher into a flow of the gifts of the Holy Spirit.

Never allow the importance of your music ministry to be diminished in your mind. Always be conscious that your ministry is to "...sing unto the Lord a new song, and his praise in the congregation of saints" (Psalm 149:1).

A FINAL WORD

Wow! Do you still think you want to be in the traveling ministry? Studying the full picture of what the traveling ministry really entails, it is evident that the traveling ministry requires just as much commitment as any other type of ministry, including pastoral ministry. As you can see by what you have read, there is a lot more to the traveling ministry than just "have Bible, will travel."

It's important to realize that most of the things a traveling minister has to deal with are outside of the pulpit. Whether in the pulpit or out, you must be diligent about your calling. How you conduct your ministry outside of the pulpit will greatly determine how successful your ministry will be.

Remember, the traveling ministry is a multi-faceted ministry. Administration, marketing, traveling, scheduling, designing and developing new products, dealing with legal concerns, financial decisions, and preaching the Word of God are just some of the things you have to be concerned about. In the beginning, you may have to wear many hats to make sure your ministry is conducted in an excellent manner.

In the traveling ministry, issues of excellence, ethics, and integrity are paramount in any decision you make. Conducting yourself above reproach and in a godly manner will cause others to receive you favorably. I encourage you to make the decision that as a traveling minister you will never conduct yourself unethically or be involved in anything that is questionable or inappropriate.

There may be times when you would rather be doing something else, but if God called you to go to the world and minister the Gospel, the grace of God will enable you to fulfill the call. When God sends you out, He will also supply every need as you are willing and obedient to do His will.

The traveling ministry is one of the highest callings a person could ever receive. As a traveling minister, you are a valuable part of the Body of Christ. I want to pray for you as you strive to be the minister God has called you to be, traveling the path He has ordained for your life.

Heavenly Father, I pray for my fellow ministers as they obey Your call and go into a lost and dying world with the message of Jesus Christ. May they always remember the call You have placed upon their lives and that You, the Almighty God, have anointed and equipped them to do the work of the ministry. I pray that they bear much fruit, walk in Your ways, and allow You to work through them in a mighty way. Bless their families, Lord, and supply their every need according to Your abundance. Give them the peace that comes with knowing that they are in the perfect will of God, doing what You have called them to do. Amen.